The ocean covers nearly
71 percent of planet Earth.

EXTREME OCEAN

OCEAN

AMAZING ANIMALS, HIGH-TECH GEAR, RECORD-BREAKING DEPTHS, AND MUCH MORE!

SYLVIA A. EARLE

AND GLEN PHELAN

ROCKFORD PUBLIC LIBRARY

NATIONAL GEOGRAPHIC

WASHINGTON, D.C.

Since 1888, the National Geographic Society has
funded more than 12,000 research, exploration, and
preservation projects around the world. The Society
receives funds from National Geographic Partners,
LLC, funded in part by your purchase. A portion of
the proceeds from this book supports this vital work.
To learn more, visit natgeo.com/info.

For more information, visit nationalgeographic.com,
call 1-877-873-6846, or write to the following address:

National Geographic Partners
1145 17th Street N.W.
Washington, DC 20036-4688 U.S.A.

Visit us online at nationalgeographic.com/books

For librarians and teachers: ngchildrensbooks.org

More for kids from National Geographic:
natgeokids.com

National Geographic Kids magazine inspires children to
explore their world with fun yet educational articles
on animals, science, nature, and more. Using fresh
storytelling and amazing photography, *Nat Geo Kids*
shows kids ages 6 to 14 the fascinating truth about the
world—and why they should care.
kids.nationalgeographic.com/subscribe

For information about special discounts for bulk
purchases, please contact National Geographic
Books Special Sales: specialsales@natgeo.com

For rights or permissions inquiries, please contact
National Geographic Books Subsidiary Rights:
bookrights@natgeo.com

SPONSORED BY

THE
PHILIP
STEPHENSON
FOUNDATION

The Philip Stephenson Foundation is dedicated to
advancing ocean exploration, conservation, and
security. We are proud to partner with National
Geographic to sponsor Dr. Sylvia A. Earle's latest
book in the hope that young readers join her in
becoming stewards of our oceans.

Designed by James Hiscott, Jr.

The publisher would like to thank Paige Towler, project
editor; Julide Dengel, art director; Kelley Miller, photo
editor; Sarah J. Mock, senior photo editor; Jennifer Kelly
Geddes, fact-checker; Joan Gossett, editorial production
manager; and Anne LeongSon and Gus Tello, design
production assistants. Special thanks to the Philip
Stephenson Foundation for their invaluable support.

Library of Congress Cataloging-in-Publication Data
Names: Earle, Sylvia A., 1935- author. | Phelan, Glen,
    author.
Title: Extreme ocean / by Sylvia Earle with Glen Phelan.
Description: Washington, DC : National Geographic Kids,
    [2020] | Audience: Ages: 8-12. | Audience: Grades: 4-6.
Identifiers: LCCN 2019007815 | ISBN 9781426336850
    (pbk.) | ISBN 9781426336867(hardcover)
Subjects: LCSH: Ocean—Juvenile literature.
Classification: LCC GC21.5 .E37 2020 | DDC 551.46—dc23
LC record available at https://lccn.loc.gov/2019007815

Printed in China
19/PPS/1

Manta rays / Hanifaru Bay, Maldives

The remains of a roller coaster in New Jersey, U.S.A., after Hurricane Sandy.

CONTENTS

INTRODUCTION

I DON'T KNOW HOW MANY fins there were. Fifty? Sixty? ... A hundred? It was impossible to count as the triangular structures sliced gracefully through the water, just above the surface, in every direction. Through the clear Gulf of Mexico water, I could see that those fins belonged to the largest fish in the sea—whale sharks.

I watched with awe as dozens of these bus-size giants glided near the surface, sucking up plankton and small fish like industrial-strength vacuum cleaners. I was surprised by their grace and precision.

The ocean is like that—full of surprises. As a scientist and explorer, I have spent more than 7,000 hours beneath the waves. That's almost 292 days! Whether scuba diving in the sunlit waters above a coral reef or piloting a submersible through the dark ocean depths, I see things I've never seen before. (Often, I see things no one has seen before.)

In this book, I'll share with you some amazing experiences from my ocean explorations. You'll find out what it's like to come eye to eye with a humpback whale, to live underwater for days at a time, and to walk on the ocean floor deeper than anyone has gone.

That's not all. You'll learn all about the ocean and its wonders. You'll find out how the ocean benefits you even if you never set foot in it. You'll discover creatures you may have never imagined—a kaleidoscope of colors and shapes. You'll get to know some of these watery inhabitants up close and personal as we discover who's who in the deep blue—like seahorses, garibaldi, giant isopods, sea butterflies, and many, many more. Together we'll explore the habitats of these creatures and see how behaviors that may seem quirky to us help these animals survive.

And what about the marvelous machines that carry us to the ocean's depths? You'll find out how engineers and technicians have built submersibles and other tools that have opened up this wondrous watery world to scientists ... and to you.

The ocean is immense. Yet it's not immune to the actions of humans. At the very moment that the whale sharks were swimming around me in the clear Gulf waters, elsewhere in the Gulf, oil was gushing out of a busted well on the seafloor, endangering every living thing that makes the Gulf its home. This book will help you understand how the ocean is hurting. But there is hope! It's not too late to save the blue heart of the planet—the life-giving ocean. You'll see how young people like you are doing just that.

Let's dive in and explore the deep blue wilderness.

—*Sylvia A. Earle*

Sylvia A. Earle poses inside a submersible.

Lemonpeel angelfish / Huahine, French Polynesia

8

CHAPTER I

>>> Blue Heart of the Planet

X

[OCEAN—Immense body of salt water
that covers nearly three-fourths
of Earth's surface]

A wave crashes off the island of Oahu, in Hawaii, U.S.A.

ROGUE WAVE!

I NEVER SAW IT COMING.

I STOOD KNEE-DEEP IN THE OCEAN WATCHING A GENTLE WAVE THAT HAD JUST PASSED ME ROLL TOWARD SHORE.

I was just a toddler, playing with my family on a summer day at a beach in New Jersey, U.S.A. The sun was hot and I was having fun splashing in the cool water along the shoreline. I had never experienced anything quite like it. In fact, everything about this beach adventure was new to me.

I remember how the adventure began, walking over sand dunes toward the ocean. Before I could see the ocean, I could hear it, the rhythmic *whoosh ... whoosh ... whoosh* of the waves mixed with the *kow, kow, kow* of gulls and the chatter of other shorebirds.

Sylvia A. Earle, middle, with her brothers, Skip and Evan

The air had a wild, fresh smell, and I could taste the salty spray blown by the wind off the tops of breaking waves somewhere in the distance.

Finally, as I reached the top of the last dune, there it was—the ocean. I could see it! And in a few minutes, I would be able to touch it! I could barely contain myself.

I remember the thrill of stepping into the edge of the surf for the first time. Wave after wave crashed, tumbled, and flowed over the sand like clear liquid glass. The surf washed over my feet, squishing sand between my toes.

Everything was exciting and new. I picked up tiny seashells that seemed to be painted in an endless variety of colors and swirling patterns. I watched little sand crabs skitter this way and that. Green seaweed wriggled like ribbons with the water's motion.

Gradually, I waded deeper, enjoying the feel of the cool ocean lapping against my knees. I jumped as each wave approached. The top of the wave sometimes reached my waist before slipping away and continuing toward the shore.

That's where I was gazing, my back to the ocean, when suddenly I was swept off my feet. A rogue wave—a large wave that forms unexpectedly—had just slammed into me!

Nearly twice my height, the wave knocked me upside down. Its swirling motion held me underwater. I was helpless to fight its power as it rolled and tumbled me like a stone. I didn't know which way was up. The only sound was a muffled *VOOOSH!* Worst of all, I couldn't breathe! I wanted air, but there was none.

Then, as quickly as the wave arrived, it passed. The water subsided, my toes touched bottom, and I realized that I was OK.

More than OK—I was exhilarated! I discovered that tumbling around underwater was really fun!

My mother noticed. No one would have blamed her if she had scooped me up and kept me from going near the ocean ever again. But she saw the big smile on my face, and instead of taking me out of the water, she let me jump right back in.

That was the day I fell in love with the ocean. I was three years old, and I have been "jumping right back in" ever since.

Notes From the Field

I HAVE SPENT MUCH OF MY LIFE exploring the ocean, sharing my experiences, and helping protect the many creatures that live in the sea. But as a young child, I wasn't very helpful to my favorite ocean animal at the time—the horseshoe crab. With its large rounded shell as big as a dinner plate, jointed legs, and long spiky tail, it was unlike anything I had ever seen. Each summer thousands of them crawled ashore. I worried that they would die out of the water, so one by one I picked them up and set them back in the ocean. What I didn't know is that they were climbing up the beach to lay and fertilize eggs in the wet sand before returning to the sea. No wonder they kept coming ashore no matter how often I "saved" them!

A diver explores the underwater landscape.

the GLOBAL OCEAN

PICTURE THIS: YOU GIVE A GLOBE A GOOD SPIN, CLOSE YOUR EYES, AND THEN STOP THE GLOBE BY PRESSING ON IT WITH A FINGER. Do you think your finger is more likely to be pointing to water or land? A glance at the map on these pages gives the answer. The ocean covers nearly 71 percent of our planet, making your finger much more likely to point to something blue than something brown, black, or green.

Where did all this water come from? No one knows for sure, but evidence indicates that a lot of it came from outer space. It wasn't like a huge cosmic rainstorm. Instead, over millions of years, the water hitched a ride on comets, meteors, and meteorites—bits of space rocks ranging from as small as a speck of dust to bigger than a house.

Many of these rocks had water molecules inside, like a bunch of tiny chocolate chips scattered throughout a cookie. Some of the meteorites were up to 22 percent water, just like a lot of meteorites today!

Scientists think that about 4.6 billion years ago, these waterlogged meteorites, along with other rocky material, began colliding and attaching to one another.

SLAM! SMASH! BANG! Bit by bit, chunk by chunk, the rocks glommed on to one another and formed a growing ball.

The result? Earth!

At first, Earth was so hot that much of the water vaporized. But as the planet cooled, the vapor became liquid and rained back to Earth, forming the ocean.

Who would have guessed that our sparkling blue waters came from the black depths of space!

ONE OCEAN

CONTINENTS PARTLY SEPARATE the global ocean into four regions that geographers call the Atlantic, Pacific, Indian, and Arctic Oceans. But they are all part of one vast watery world that is full of life, mystery, and wonder.

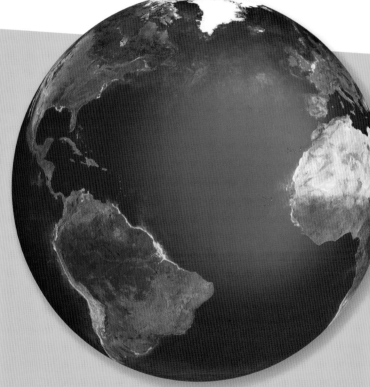

DEPTH
The ocean is deep. It averages 2.6 miles (4.2 km) in depth, but some of it is three times deeper!

LIFE
The ocean is full of life of enormous variety. From the shallow reefs to the deepest trenches, sea creatures of nearly every imaginable shape, size, and color, like this dragonet mandarin, have adapted to thrive in widely varied environments.

LIGHT
Sunlight brightens the first few hundred feet of the ocean. But the deeper you go, the darker it gets. At around 2,000 feet (610 m), the ocean is dark, both day and night. Think of it! All creatures in the sea live in the dark some of the time, but most of them live in the dark all of the time!

SALINITY
The ocean is salty. In fact, a gallon (3.8 L) of ocean salt water contains up to 4.7 ounces (133 g) of salt. Most of the salt is washed from the land by rivers and streams that flow into the sea, but some is also added by mineral-rich volcanic springs deep within the sea.

Portland Head Lighthouse in Cape Elizabeth, Maine, U.S.A.

AN OCEAN IN MOTION

TINY RIPPLES SPREAD ACROSS A QUIET BAY, lapping gently against the rocky shoreline. At the same instant, far

out at sea, towering walls of water crash down on the decks of a cargo ship as the huge steel craft helplessly rides out a storm.

What do these events have in common? They both show that the ocean is in constant motion. In these cases, that motion is caused by waves. And most waves, no matter their size, form the same way—by wind blowing across the water. The energy of the wind moves from the air to the water and creates waves. It's like blowing on a bowl of hot soup. The energy in the blowing air moves to the soup and makes little ripples—waves.

NATURE'S SIGNAL

the bottoms and eventually lean forward, curl, and topple over. That's when a wave "breaks."

I had plenty of opportunity to learn about waves firsthand when our family moved from a farm in New Jersey to the west coast of Florida, U.S.A. I was 12 years old, and the ocean became my backyard and my playground.

I grew up experiencing the motions of the sea, including tides. These are the daily rising and falling of water along the coast. Low tide was my favorite. With the water's edge farther from shore for a couple hours, I could roam the exposed ocean bottom, finding crabs and other animals.

Of course, the best times were in the water. But I had to watch out for the unexpected. Waves could kick up quickly and toss me about like a cork. Larger waves, like the one that toppled me when I was three, could come out of nowhere. So could strong currents.

I'm talking about rip currents. These fast-moving jets of water can form as water moves along the shoreline and then rushes back out to sea, often through a narrow break in a sandbar.

I came to recognize rip currents and learned that if I got caught in one, I should swim parallel to the shoreline. A rip current is narrow, no more than 80 feet (24.5 m) wide. So once you swim out of it, you can head back toward shore.

Waves, tides, and currents show that the ocean is constantly changing. These motions also make the ocean a wonderfully extreme environment, as you'll see throughout this book.

As you stand on shore and watch the waves roll in, it might look like the water is rolling toward you. But only the energy in the form of the waves is moving toward you. The water itself just bobs up and down as the energy passes through ... until the wave hits the shore.

In the shallow water near shore, the bottoms of the waves begin to touch the sloping ocean floor. Friction with the floor slows the waves but also pushes them higher. The wave tops move faster than

WHAT GOOD IS THE OCEAN?

ALL LIFE REQUIRES WATER.

Ninety-seven percent of Earth's water is ocean. Not surprisingly, that is where most living things exist. But land dwellers, including people, are connected to the sea, too. Even if you live far from the coast and never touch the ocean, the ocean touches you with every breath you take and every drop of water you drink. In a way, we are all sea creatures, as dependent on the ocean as whales, sea stars, and coral reefs!

Take a deep breath ... This simple act would not be possible without the ocean. Air is made mostly of a gas called nitrogen, and small amounts of carbon dioxide and other gases, but about 21 percent is oxygen. That's the gas that moves from your lungs to your blood and then throughout your body to make everything work. We couldn't live without oxygen, and guess where more than half of it comes from. That's right—the ocean!

The sunlit waters near the surface are loaded with tiny organisms called phytoplankton. Like trees, grass, and other plants on land, phytoplankton capture sunlight, carbon dioxide gas, and water to make sugar. In this way, phytoplankton are like little food factories. The sugar becomes food for themselves and for the animals that eat them.

1-2-3 WATER!

HERE'S SOMETHING ELSE the ocean provides—freshwater! How can that be when ocean water is salty? Simple. The ocean is a major part of the water cycle.

1. Water constantly evaporates from the ocean.
2. The salt stays behind as the water vapor rises in the air, cools, and condenses as clouds.
3. The water droplets that make up the clouds may eventually fall as rain. Some of the clouds blow over land and produce rain that falls into rivers and lakes and soaks into the ground, providing the freshwater we drink.

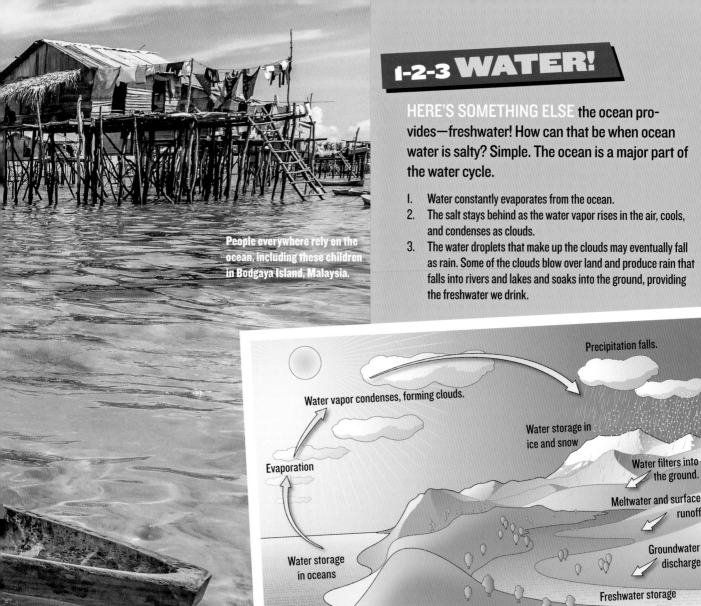

Precipitation falls.

Water vapor condenses, forming clouds.

Water storage in ice and snow

Evaporation

Water filters into the ground.

Meltwater and surface runoff

Groundwater discharge

Water storage in oceans

Freshwater storage

This process of food production is called photosynthesis. During this process, phytoplankton release oxygen into the ocean and into the air above. So you connect with the ocean every time you breathe!

To understand another way the ocean affects your life, think about filling a bathtub. The water pouring from the faucet is nice and warm, but by the time it collects in the back of the tub, it has cooled off a bit.

How do you keep the entire tub of water warm? One way is to make a current. Sitting in the tub facing the faucet, you might pull water toward you with your left hand while pushing water away from you with your right. The current that you make transfers heat evenly around the tub. It's not too hot by your feet and not too cool by your back.

Currents in the ocean have a similar effect but on a global scale. Driven by the wind, they are shaped by the terrain, by differences in temperature and salinity, and by the motion of the turning Earth. These currents move tremendous volumes of surface water in circular pathways around the globe, transferring heat from the warm tropics to the cold polar regions. This transfer of heat affects the general climate of an area as well as its day-to-day weather.

The ocean also moderates our planet's temperature by absorbing much of the sun's heat. Think of it! Without the ocean, Earth would be uninhabitable—too hot, too dry, and with an atmosphere lacking the oxygen needed to support life as we know it.

In short, the ocean makes life on Earth possible.

THE OCEAN SEEMED TO BE BREATHING.

I was standing on the very edge of an ice shelf surrounding the continent of Antarctica. Most of the land here is covered by ice about one mile (1.6 km) thick. This huge expanse of ice formed slowly over time as the year-round cold weather prevented snow from melting. Year after year, snow built up. The weight of top layers compressed the bottom layers into dense ice. Over hundreds of thousands of years, an ice sheet formed.

Beneath the Antarctic ice sheet lies solid bedrock. But not where I stood.

I was on an expedition as chief scientist for the National Oceanic and Atmospheric Administration, or NOAA. I had just landed by helicopter near the edge of the Ross Ice Shelf. This relatively thin, broad platform of ice extends for miles from Antarctica over the surrounding ocean. From the air, the ice shelf looked like a vast plain of brilliant white marble—sturdy and still.

Standing on it was quite another matter.

Near the land, the ice extends down for thousands of feet. But at the edge, the ice is only a few feet thick. It lifts and lowers gently with the rhythm of the ocean beyond. I felt like I was standing on a sleeping whale, rising and falling with each heaving breath!

As I looked out from the fragile shelf, I thought about the importance of ice on the ocean. Ice sheets cover not only Antarctica near the South Pole but also Greenland near the North Pole. In both regions, huge slabs of sea ice cover much of the ocean.

Polar ice is tied directly to the health of the ocean and our planet. Because ice is white, it reflects much

AN OCEAN OF ICE

Ross Ice Shelf / Antarctica

of the sunlight that strikes it. This reflection, along with the low angle of the sun, keeps the polar water and air cold. Ocean and air currents circulate that cold water and air around the globe. As a result, most of our planet is not too hot and not too cold.

Without the ice, the darker land and sea would absorb the sunlight, become warmer, and warm the air above. Climates would change around the world, especially near the poles. As you'll find out in chapter 4, such change is already happening.

Ice on the land and sea also supports wildlife. I was reminded of that fact as I stared out to sea deep in thought.

Without warning, a penguin rocketed out of the ocean and landed with two padded feet on the ice. Then ... *PHOOM! PHOOM!* Out popped another and another until a dozen or so black-and-white Adélie penguins, each about two feet (0.6 m) tall, had propelled themselves from the water onto the ice.

As each penguin gained its footing, it ran right toward me. And by ran I mean waddled really fast.

With their wings sticking out and their small bodies rocking back and forth, they reminded me of human toddlers taking their first steps.

Clumsy as they looked, the penguins were much more sure-footed on the ice than I was. When only a few feet away, they came to an abrupt halt. They stared. I stared.

For several minutes, the penguins sized me up. Then they waddled off, sometimes sliding on their belly instead, before diving back into the sea.

Long before humans existed, penguins thrived in Antarctica. The continent wasn't even glimpsed by a human—a Russian explorer—until 1820. Even now, most of the region is unexplored, both above and below the ocean. No wonder the penguins were curious about the strange creature—me—that had arrived on their icy doorstep!

Adélie penguins / Ross Sea, Antarctica

Who's Who / Penguin

PENGUINS ARE AT HOME IN ANTARCTICA. Dense layers of feathers and a layer of fat provide insulation against the extreme cold air and water. Unlike most birds, they can't fly, but they are fantastic swimmers. Their sleek shape helps them move swiftly and gracefully through the water. When they want to get out of the water, they usually don't climb out—they shoot out! Underwater, a penguin builds up speed and releases a stream of bubbles from its body. The bubbles create a tunnel of air that allows the penguin to triple its speed, enough to launch itself out of the water and onto the ice.

Ruins caused by a tsunami in Sumatra, Indonesia

THAT'S EXTREME: TSUNAMI

ON DECEMBER 26, 2004, disaster struck in the Indian Ocean. Two huge sections of Earth's rocky crust beneath the seafloor suddenly slipped past each other off the coast of the island of Sumatra, Indonesia. As a result, a slab of ocean floor nearly as long as the U.S. state of California was violently thrust upward a whopping 65 feet (20 m); imagine the height of 10 tall adults standing on each other's shoulders!

The shock waves from this sudden release of energy shook that part of the globe in one of the world's strongest recorded earthquakes. An even more extreme event followed.

The upward thrust of the seafloor sent pulses of energy through the water above it. These pulses created a series of waves called a tsunami. The waves were barely noticeable at sea as they raced across the ocean with the speed of a jet airliner. But by the time the first one reached the coast, it was a wall of water 30 feet (9 m) tall!

The incredible force of the water smashed boats in harbors, poured over protective walls, and flooded towns more than two miles (3.2 km) inland.

Within minutes, a second monster wave hit, then a third. The water that drained back toward the sea carried with it the debris of buildings, boats, and vehicles.

Tragically, more than 150,000 people lost their lives, making it one of the world's deadliest tsunamis.

The tsunami was no ordinary wave, and it wasn't made in an ordinary way.

Unlike the typical surface waves that are driven by the wind, tsunamis form by a disturbance from below. The disturbance is usually from an earthquake, but it might also be from an underwater landslide or volcanic eruption.

Tsunamis are infrequent, and most are small. However, they can cause extreme destruction to coastal communities. Luckily, scientists are developing better warning systems and safety campaigns.

NATURE'S SIGNAL

SOMETIMES RIGHT BEFORE a tsunami strikes, the water along the shore is pulled out to sea, exposing the seafloor and stranding boats. This occurs when the trough, or low point, of the tsunami wave reaches shore before the wave's crest, or high point. Water is sucked away from the shore. This is a sign that the damaging crest of the tsunami is only a few minutes behind. Such was the case in many places along shores during the Indonesian tsunami of 2004.

HOW TO MODEL OCEAN WAVES

YOU'VE PROBABLY MADE WAVES
lots of times, from splashing in a pool to throwing stones in a pond to blowing on hot soup. But how do those waves affect things in and on the water? How do the waves change as they move through the water? It's easy to find out.

MATERIALS

- Long, narrow container (Try a rectangular baking dish or roasting pan.)
- Object that floats (cork, toy boat)
- Rocks

STEPS

1. Place the container on a flat surface.

2. Fill the container with water about two-thirds of the way.

3. Place a floating object in the water.

4. Wait for the water to be still. Then make gentle waves by pressing the flat of your hand once against the water's surface at one end of the container. Watch how the object moves.

5. Make a model shoreline by placing rocks at one end of the container. Start placing the rocks about one-fourth the distance from the end. Then add rocks so that the "ocean bottom" slopes upward toward the "shore" and rises above water at the end.

6. Make a wave at the other end and watch how it changes as it nears the shore.

7. Think of other ways to experiment with waves in your model ocean. Try using different toys or containers, or building different types of shores. Be sure to clean up any spills right away.

1

2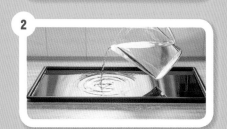

3

4

5

6

7

CHAPTER 2

LIFE
Beneath the Waves

>>>

X

[BIODIVERSITY—The variety of living things in an ecosystem
CORAL REEF—An ecosystem growing on the seafloor and made up of living corals, their skeletons, and many other kinds of organisms
ECOSYSTEM—The living and nonliving things in an area and their interactions]

A harp seal swimming in ice-filled water, Gulf of St. Lawrence, Canada

EYE TO EYE WITH GIANTS

Humpback whales,
mother and calf

IT LOOKED LIKE A BUS SPEEDING THROUGH WATER,

and it was coming straight at me! There was no time to move. What would happen next? I had no idea, but one thing was certain: I could not survive a collision with an animal that outweighed me by 80,000 pounds (36,287 kg)!

For a moment, I wondered whether our plan to observe whales up close was really a good idea. For months I had been hoping to be right here—suspended in warm, blue water several miles off the coast of Maui, Hawaii, U.S.A. Why? To observe humpback whales. I wanted to find out what they do in the place where they spend most of their lives—under the sea.

Until then, most of what we knew about these ocean giants we learned by seeing them when they came to the surface to breathe. Or when they were dead, cast ashore or hunted by whalers to be used for food, oil, and other products.

But I wanted to watch them swim with their families. I wanted to be there as they descended into depths far beyond where people can go—all on a single breath of air!

I especially wanted to hear them sing. After all, humpbacks are known as the "singing whales."

As a scientist, I was on assignment for *National Geographic* magazine to report on the discoveries that our small team was making about these magnificent creatures. Our main goal was to record humpback whale songs and try to link the whales' sounds with their actions. We had located a group of five humpbacks swimming not far from our small rubber boat. This was our chance!

Photographers Al Giddings and Chuck Nicklin and I lowered ourselves into the water. We were now in the whales' world and about to get to know them up close and personal.

I peered through my mask, trying to see as far as possible into the infinite blueness. Several minutes went by. Then ... there it was!

Fuzzy at first, the outline sharpened quickly as the dark shape of a female humpback rushed toward me. The whale's movements, which had seemed slow and lumbering on the water's surface, now appeared frighteningly fast. I froze as the whale loomed larger and larger. She was now only a few yards away. A collision was all but certain.

Then, at the last instant, the enormous mammal twisted her large fin ever so slightly and turned just enough to miss me. As she swept past, our eyes met. Hers—the size of a grapefruit—moved side to side to get a good look at this strange being with four limbs and a cylinder on its back. Then she continued toward Al, lifting one of her immense flippers up and over his head to avoid a collision.

The whale and her four companions moved underwater as gracefully as ballet dancers. They twisted, turned, swerved, and rolled like underwater acrobats. When they swam close by, we could see them eyeing us. It seemed that they were as curious about us as we were about them!

The whales stayed with us for nearly three hours. Sometimes they plunged deep, disappearing into the dark waters below for several minutes. Then they suddenly reappeared, shooting to the surface to take a breath.

Weeks later, we encountered a singing whale. Even before we saw him, we felt the sound. Then, through the shimmering blue, the dark shape of the whale came into focus. He seemed to be standing on his head, flippers extended like wings. His deep rumbles shifted to birdlike chirps and rippling notes that resembled the sounds from a flute, then a violin, and then a donkey!

This roller coaster of sound repeated in cycles, each lasting about 20 minutes. It was hauntingly beautiful—rivaling any symphony I've ever heard.

THE HUMPBACK is only one of many kinds of whales that live in the ocean. Whales are the giants of the sea. Humpbacks are as big as a bus. Read on to find out more about these gentle giants.

Humpbacks have **BALEEN PLATES** instead of teeth. Baleen looks like a row of brushes hanging down from the roof of the mouth. The whale takes a big gulp of water and forces it out through the baleen. Tasty morsels like krill and small fish get caught in the baleen. Then the whale swallows them down.

Whales are mammals, and like all mammals, they have some hair and warm bodies, and they nurse their young. They also have lungs and breathe air. A whale inhales and exhales through its **BLOWHOLE**. Water vapor in the air from the lungs condenses when it meets the cooler outside air and forms a misty spray. After exhaling, the whale breathes in fresh air through the opening before diving underwater. The blowhole closes to keep water out. When diving deep for food, most whales can hold their breath for a half hour or more.

The **PECTORAL FINS** are each nearly one-third the length of the body. They are like wings and help the whale move in the water.

AN OCEAN OF LIFE

THE GREATEST DIVERSITY OF LIFE ON EARTH IS IN THE OCEAN.

Microscopic animals made of only one cell share the waters with the largest animals ever known. But the ocean has many kinds of environments, and each is occupied by different kinds of life.

SUNLIT ZONE

0–660 feet (0–200 m)

Sunshine lights up the top layer. The sunlight provides the energy that phytoplankton use to produce food during photosynthesis. These microscopic organisms form the basis of systems of food chains that sustain the majority of the ocean's animals.

TWILIGHT ZONE

660–1,800 feet (200–550 m)

Only a small amount of sunlight reaches this depth. Without the warmth of the sun, the water temperature drops steadily to a chilly 46°F (8°C), even in the tropics. Animals here generally have larger eyes and other structures to capture what little light there is. Many also have body parts that glow like a firefly. This trait has a fancy name—bioluminescence (pronounced bye-oh-loom-i-NES-uns). The light can lure prey, frighten predators, or attract mates or companions.

Within this zone, the largest migrations on Earth take place: Massive bands of squid, small fish, crustaceans, jellyfish, and other kinds of animals move up from the depths at night to graze on the plankton that have generated food during the daytime. As dawn approaches, these enormous gatherings of animals move back into the darkness below, where predators are less likely to find them.

MIDNIGHT ZONE

1,800–13,100 feet (550–4,000 m)

This part of the ocean is dark and cold, about 39°F (4°C). Most creatures in this zone have some form of bioluminescence.

At this depth, pressure from the weight of the water would crush a human. That's because people have air-filled structures like lungs and sinuses, and the weight of the water compresses the air in their bodies.

ABYSSAL ZONE

13,100–19,700 feet (4,000–6,000 m)

The average depth of the ocean—2.6 miles (4.2 km)—is encompassed in this zone.

Temperatures at the bottom of the abyssal zone hover just above freezing. This is an extreme environment for humans, but life abounds here.

Many of the organisms that live here feed on bits of dead plants and animals that drift down from above, called marine snow. In certain places, hot water flowing beneath the seafloor erupts into springs called hydrothermal vents. This hot water is loaded with minerals and gases. Certain microbes, bacteria, and microscopic creatures called Archaea use some of these gases instead of light to make food during a process called chemosynthesis.

HADAL ZONE

19,700–35,827 feet (6,000–10,920 m)

This immense zone encompasses an area larger than the United States or China and includes dozens of trenches. These are the deepest, least explored places on Earth.

Only two expeditions have taken people to the deepest trench nearly seven miles (11.3 km) down. What have researchers found there? Life! So far, discoveries include a flounder-like fish, sea cucumbers, microbes, and tracks of burrowing animals. But we've spent only a few hours looking. Think of how much more there is to be discovered!

How whales dive so deep!

Many kinds of whales can dive into the twilight zone or beyond in search of food. But how can they survive at those depths? What happens when the air in their lungs compresses under the crushing pressure? The answers lie in some incredible adaptations. Right before a whale takes a long deep dive, it folds down its rib cage and collapses its lungs, squeezing out almost all the air. The whale's heart rate lowers and other organs and systems slow or shut down, conserving the oxygen that remains in its body. Its shrunken lungs make the whale less buoyant, so it glides down with little effort. Some whales may stay submerged for an hour, using bursts of sound to find and then feast on squid and other creatures that live in the deep-sea darkness.

NAME THAT FISH!

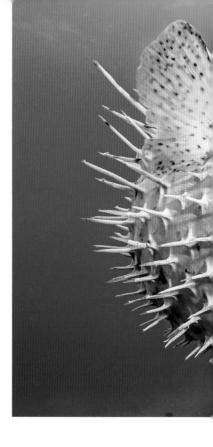

LIFE HAS ADAPTED to every place and every set of conditions the vast ocean has to offer. As a result, the ocean's creatures are as varied and interesting as their names. You might be familiar with a porcupine, but how about a porcupinefish? Or a raccoon butterflyfish? What do you think these creatures look like? See if you can match each ocean animal name on page 31 with the correct picture. Answers are at the bottom of the page.

SO, HOW DID YOU DO?
DID YOU RECOGNIZE THE CONNECTIONS BETWEEN THE NAME AND THE ANIMAL?

These weird fish names are clues to the incredible variety of life, or biodiversity, in the world's ocean. Pick any animal (or object) and chances are there's a fish that resembles it in some way! And just like animals on land are adapted to life in a forest, desert, or grassland, every ocean animal has features that make it well suited for life in the sea.

The sharp spines of a porcupinefish serve the same purpose as the quills of a porcupine—to keep the animal from being eaten. Even the hungriest predator might not want to chomp down on a ball of spikes!

And like butterflies, the nearly 125 different species of butterflyfish use their bright colors and striking patterns to attract mates or scare off predators. The raccoon butterflyfish shown here sports a black mask similar to that of the furry woodland mammal. The mask hides the fish's eyes, which might fool an attacker from knowing which end is which!

Now, take another look at the pineapplefish. If you've ever seen a whole pineapple, the pattern on this fish's body should look familiar. But the similarities don't stop there. The tough yellow scales on the fish are lined with protective spines, just like the tough skin and spines on a pineapple protect the juicy fruit inside.

Does the shape of the guitarfish remind you of its namesake? The fish's wide, flat body makes it easier to bury itself in the sandy or muddy bottom and snack on the worms and crabs that wander by.

You might be wondering, "Hmm ... are any other fish named after musical instruments?" Of course! Besides guitarfish, a dive in shallow waters might bring you face to face with long slim flutefish, cornetfish, or trumpetfish. If you hear a croaking or thumping sound, it may be a male drum trying to attract a mate. This fish produces a drumbeat by vibrating certain muscles against its swim bladder. The bladder is a gas-filled sac that helps the fish stay buoyant, or float at different levels in the water.

Is there a keyboard fish to round out the undersea orchestra? Not that we have found yet, but who knows what wondrous creatures remain to be discovered.

WHICH FISH IS WHICH?

Guitarfish

Porcupinefish

Raccoon butterflyfish

Pineapplefish

A. Porcupinefish, B. Raccoon butterflyfish, C. Guitarfish, D. Pineapplefish

Sea anemone

Grey Plover

SHORE
Life

A tide pool at low tide in
British Columbia, Canada

LOW TIDE
HAS ALWAYS BEEN MY FAVORITE.

When the water recedes, a whole new beach is exposed, and there's more to explore. Dozens of plovers, sandpipers, and other shorebirds scurry across the exposed beach. Each one stops now and then to jab its long beak into the soft sand. Burrowing crabs, worms, and mollusks that dine on plankton and other small animals become meals themselves for the hungry birds.

Avoiding predators isn't the only challenge for animals living along the shore. Waves crash, churning up sand and hurling stones. The tide comes and goes. Land that is covered with cool water in the morning may dry out and bake in the hot afternoon sun.

Yet life is plentiful here. The tide brings in a hearty soup of plankton and other small organisms. Places that are harsh to some creatures provide exactly what others need to prosper. This is certainly true in the intertidal zone—the area between high and low tide. Hard-shelled mussels and limpets cling to rocks. So do many kinds of seaweed as well as sea anemones and numerous other animals.

At low tide, these creatures respond to the lack of water. Anemones fold up like a ball. Seaweeds shrink. Mussels and limpets close their shells to avoid drying out in the open air and wind. On the sandy beach, crabs and clams dig down to stay moist and out of sight of hungry animals. It doesn't always work, though. The holes the shellfish make sometimes give away their hiding places!

Some of the most challenging habitats along the shore are also some of the most interesting to explore—tide pools. These small rocky enclosures trap seawater and lots of sea life during low tide. In some ways, a tide pool is like an outdoor aquarium.

Some tide pool organisms are permanent residents. Barnacles, sponges, and most anemones spend their adult lives in one spot. Others, such as urchins, snails, crabs, fish, and the occasional octopus, are only visitors, waiting for high tide to carry them over the rock walls. Some of these animals return to the pool as the tide moves out.

What makes tide pools such tough places to live? Most are only a few feet deep, so on a hot day, the water heats up noticeably and holds less oxygen. Some of the water evaporates, which increases the salinity (how much salt there is) of what remains. Organisms that have adapted to such extreme changes in their surroundings thrive in these shoreline habitats.

>>> BET YOU DIDN'T KNOW ...

What causes tides!

The tides are caused mostly by gravity—that invisible force that makes all objects pull on one another. The moon's gravity is especially important in governing the tides. The moon's gravity pulls the water facing the moon into a slight bulge. Another bulge of water forms on the other side of Earth because of Earth's motion in its orbit. As Earth rotates, a place along a shoreline moves into a bulge. That's when the water starts creeping up the shore and the tide "comes in," culminating in high tide. Earth continues to rotate and the same place moves out of the bulge. The tide "goes out," resulting in low tide. Some shorelines have two high tides and two low tides each day, while others have just one high tide and low tide a day.

Notes From the Field

IT'S FUN TO EXPLORE an exposed beach at low tide, but you have to be aware of when the high tide is coming back in. You don't want to become stranded on a rock and have to swim back to shore.

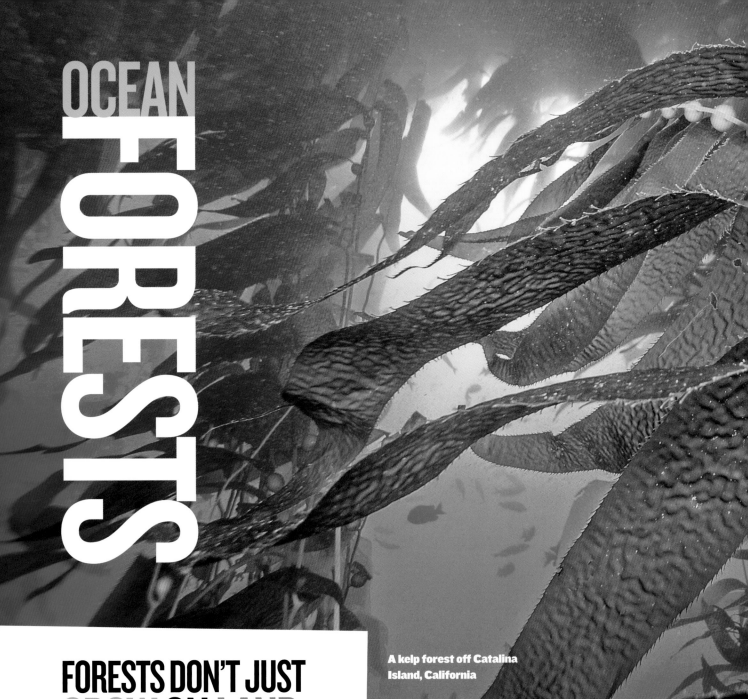

OCEAN FORESTS

A kelp forest off Catalina Island, California

FORESTS DON'T JUST GROW ON LAND;

they also grow in the ocean. And like land forests, ocean forests are giant ecosystems teeming with life! These ocean forests are not made of trees, but of several kinds of large slippery brown seaweeds called kelp.

Kelp forests grow mostly in rocky coastal areas where the cool, sunlit waters are rich in nutrients. Kelps need sunlight because, like plants, they photosynthesize to make their own food. But kelps technically are algae—not plants—even though they have parts that might remind you of their counterparts on land. For instance, at the bottom of each stalk of kelp is a rootlike bundle of strands called a holdfast. Like a root, the holdfast anchors the main stem, the stalk, to the seafloor.

Some kelps are enormous. One of the giant kelps that grow along the coast of North and South America is called macrocystis. Its towering stalks extend from the seafloor to the surface in water depths as great as 130 feet (40 m).

Long slender fronds that look like leaves extend from the stalks. Gas-filled bulbs at the base of the fronds keep the heavy stalk upright and reaching toward the

A sea otter cleans his fur with kelp.

ONE OF THE MANY RESIDENTS of a kelp forest is the garibaldi. This fish's bright orange body stands out against the brown kelp and blue-green water. The male garibaldi's behavior and personality are as colorful as his appearance. He searches the seafloor at the bottom of the forest to find sprigs of seaweed called red algae growing among the rocks. He trims the red algae by nibbling at them until sections about as long as your thumb remain—just the right size for a nest where a female can lay eggs.

A messy home won't do for this finicky fish. He keeps things tidy by eating small bits of algae and brushing away grains of sand or other debris. Then he defends his territory with attitude! He shoos away urchins or other animals that wander by. Curious divers get the heave-ho, too. When I've gotten too close, the garibaldi let me know that I am intruding by making a burping sound and bumping my face mask. And when a plump fish up to 14 inches (35.5 cm) long bumps you, you feel it!

sunlight. The stalks can grow incredibly fast—up to two feet (0.6 m) per day! That's impressive. Even more impressive are all the animals that live there.

A single frond of macrocystis kelp may be home for hundreds of tiny animals. And the masses of intertwining holdfasts provide shelter for hundreds more: mollusks, crabs, urchins, anemones, sponges, worms, and many others.

While swimming along the bottom of a kelp forest, a diver is likely to come across many round, spiny animals the size of baseballs. These are sea urchins. They graze on kelp and other algae. At the same time, urchins themselves are a vital source of food for various fish and for a very active, very furry, very whiskery, and almost always very hungry mammal—the California sea otter.

People used to hunt sea otters for their thick, soft fur and nearly drove them to extinction. As the numbers of sea otters dropped, the numbers of urchins rose. Good news for urchins; bad news for kelp. Over time, the growing populations of sea urchins consumed so much of this seaweed that the kelp forests began to decline.

Things started to turn around in the 1960s, when sea otters became protected and began to recover. Today, with more otters there are fewer urchins, and with fewer urchins, some kelp forests have rebounded.

A healthy kelp forest needs urchins and otters and the right amount of all of the creatures that live there. Eliminating any of them can cause the system to unravel or even disappear.

FIVE FRIENDLY FISH

BACKGROUND: Divers study coral near Tektite II.

TOP LEFT: Sylvia A. Earle shows an engineer her finds during a dive.

TOP RIGHT: Gray angelfish swim near a hawksbill turtle, Cozumel, Mexico.

Gear & Gadgets

THE INVENTION OF THE self-contained underwater breathing apparatus (scuba) in the 1940s enabled people to swim underwater while breathing air from a tank strapped to their back. The diver inhales air from the tank and exhales into the water creating clouds of bubbles that rise to the surface. A single tank provides enough air for a person to stay underwater for about an hour.

During the Tektite project, we often used a system called a rebreather, providing an air supply that lasts more than six hours. This system removes carbon dioxide and adds oxygen as it is consumed, releasing only occasional small bubbles. Large clouds of bubbles frighten some of the animals. But with rebreathers, the fish seemed to accept us as fellow fish!

I COULD SEE THEM GATHERING OUTSIDE

one of the bubble-shaped windows of our underwater lab. They had become a familiar sight—five gray angelfish.

From a distance, they looked solid gray except when they flapped their small pectoral fins located just behind their gills. Then, the bright yellow portion of the fins flashed against their bodies like the sun peeking through clouds.

Up close, I could see that the fish weren't solid gray at all. Rather, they were intricately patterned with tiny black ovals set in a lace of light gray. Their faces were tipped with white lips and a white chin, as if each had dipped its snout in a dish of vanilla ice cream.

Something else struck me about these five angelfish: They were all different. Every one of them had a distinctive face and a one-of-a-kind pattern of scales that marked each as an individual.

Our underwater lab, called Tektite, sat next to a reef on the sandy bottom of the Caribbean Sea, 50 feet (15 m) below the surface. In the summer of 1970, I led a team of four other aquanauts on an expedition where we lived in the habitat for two weeks. Those were two of the most important weeks of my life.

For the first time, I wasn't just visiting the ocean's creatures during a brief dive. Rather, I was living among them. Using the lab as home base, we put on our diving gear and swam for up to 12 hours a day. We did a lot of night diving, too. The water was so clear that when it was calm, we could see the moon and some of the brightest stars from our position under the sea.

Our excursions usually started right before dawn, when the sky and sea were still dark. We used flashlights to find our way to the reef. We wanted to be there at daybreak to witness how this ecosystem "wakes up." We were never disappointed.

As the sun rose and light streamed through the water, the reef seemed to come alive. It burst into a carnival of color as parrotfish, surgeonfish, angelfish, damselfish, filefish, butterflyfish, puffers, and other species that are active by day emerged from their sleeping places among the rocks and corals.

In a nearby patch of sand, a colony of garden eels greeted the new day in their own way. First, a single slender eel poked its head just above the rim of its burrow. Then up popped another, and another. Minutes later, dozens of the eels extended about half the length of their slim bodies from their burrows where they remained, anchored in the sand.

And what about the five gray angelfish? Curious and friendly, they often accompanied us as we explored the reef. As we swam together, I noticed how different they were from one another not only in appearance but also in how they behaved. It was the same thing with the barracuda, green moray eels, Nassau groupers, dog snappers, and silver tarpon. We met these animals time after time as neighbors, each with a distinctive personality, and each with its place in the coral reef system.

Those five angelfish helped me to see that, in a way, a reef is like a city. The corals are the buildings, but it takes many kinds of individuals living together to make the reef truly come alive.

37

LIFE ON A CORAL REEF

CLOWNFISH AND SEA ANEMONES A coral reef, like any ecosystem, is a battleground of competition. Organisms must compete for food, space, mates, and other resources. But there's cooperation, too. Clownfish and sea anemones are a perfect example. A clownfish produces mucus that coats its body and protects it from the anemone's poisonous tentacles. The clownfish stays safe from predators among the tentacles. In return, the feisty clownfish chases away butterflyfish, which eat anemones.

CLEANER WRASSE A fish's best friend may be a cleaner wrasse. This small fish picks off and eats parasites from a fish's gills and skin. I've seen fish actually line up, waiting their turn to be cleaned.

MORAY EEL During the day, moray eels tend to rest in the crevices between rocks or coral colonies. At night, they come out to feed. Their sharp teeth make them look fierce. But they usually prefer to stay hidden or flee if a human diver approaches.

CORAL REEFS ARE DAZZLING GARDENS OF SEA LIFE.

They form in warm, shallow, clear waters along tropical coasts and islands, and sometimes in open sea where underwater mountains rise close enough to the surface for the reefs to grow.

Coral reefs are home to at least 700 kinds of corals and 4,000 kinds of fish. There are also crabs, clams, shrimps, snails, sea stars, worms, sea turtles, sponges, and other animals that give coral reefs a greater diversity of life than any place on land. Meet a few of these amazing creatures!

GRAY REEF SHARK Many kinds of sharks patrol reefs, especially in the evening, when sharks hunt for meals. But people are not on the menu! During one dive, I swam with more than a hundred gray reef sharks. Over the years, I've encountered thousands of sharks of many different kinds, all peacefully minding their own business. As long as I didn't bother them, they didn't bother me.

PARROTFISH Parrotfish have strong front teeth that resemble a parrot's beak. They use these teeth to scrape yummy algae off the surface of coral. I've sometimes heard the scraping before I saw the fish. More teeth in the fish's throat help it chomp through chunks of coral to get to the algae and polyps inside. The fish digests the algae and polyps and expels the ground-up coral as body waste. Some of the world's most beautiful coral sand beaches are made of bits of coral that wash up on shore after parrotfish have pooped them out!

STONEFISH Many animals on a reef have body colors and patterns that help them blend in with the colorful corals and other surroundings. Such camouflage doesn't get any better than that of a stonefish. It looks like a rock covered with algae. It lies motionless on the seafloor. When an unsuspecting fish comes close by, the stonefish gobbles it up. Poisonous spines on its back protect it from predators.

CORAL POLYP A single coral animal is called a polyp. Most polyps are no bigger than the tip of your little finger. At night, these tiny animals extend tentacles that sting even tinier animals drifting by. The tentacles then bring the prey into the polyp's mouth. Polyps get food another way, too. Algae live inside the polyps. Besides giving the coral their color, the algae use sunlight to make sugars, just as plants do. The polyps use some of the sugars as food.

1-2-3 REEF-BUILDERS

YOU MIGHT THINK coral looks more like delicate rock than an animal. It's both! Here's how tiny coral polyps build huge rocky reefs.

1. Larval corals attach themselves to a hard surface, such as a rock, and grow into soft polyps.
2. The polyps use minerals in the water to form limestone cups, or skeletons, around themselves.
3. When the polyps die, the stony skeletons remain. Coral larvae attach to the skeletons and build their own on top.

Do you see a pattern emerging? Each generation of polyps grows on the limestone skeletons of the previous generation. Layer by layer, the colony grows, but only the top layer contains the live animals. Many colonies of coral form a reef. Growth is slow, from 0.2 to 4 inches (0.5–10 cm) per year. Some coral reefs have been growing for 5,000 to 10,000 years or more.

In addition to the corals, some kinds of red algae also build limestone skeletons. Many kinds look like a crust of thick pink paint growing on rocks, shells, and dead corals. Others grow upright and look like small red or pink bouquets of branches—but with no flowers!

39

LIFE IN AN EXTREME WORLD

Scientists (top) prepare to explore hydrothermal vents (background) in *Alvin*.

ON FEBRUARY 17, 1977, HISTORY WAS MADE.

A voyage to the bottom of the sea changed the way we think about life on our planet. The scientists were looking for hydrothermal vents. They thought the vents were around there somewhere. On this expedition, "somewhere" was an area along a mid-ocean ridge west of Central America. The ridge is an underwater mountain range formed over millions of years by hot, molten rock—magma—welling up from deep beneath the seafloor. The magma heats the surrounding rock. Cold seawater seeps through cracks down into the hot rock. The water heats up, rises, and spurts back into the ocean through hydrothermal vents.

Using an underwater vehicle towed behind a research vessel, the scientists took photographs that indicated the presence of what appeared to be underwater vents ... and something more! A team of two geologists and a pilot squeezed into the small research submersible, *Alvin*, and slowly descended nearly two miles (3.2 km) to the bottom of the Pacific Ocean for a better look.

The scientists were excited to explore these vents firsthand. In the glow of *Alvin*'s lights, their attention was first drawn to the black smoke billowing from rocky chimneys. They knew it wasn't smoke at all. Rather, it was a plume of minerals dissolved in water as hot as 750°F (400°C) instantly solidifying upon meeting the near-freezing seawater. Some of the solid particles built up around the opening and created the chimneys.

The vents were mesmerizing, but what the geologists saw next was mind-blowing.

One of them radioed to a colleague on a ship on the surface. "Hey, isn't the deep ocean supposed to be like a desert?"

"Yes," came the reply.

"Well, there are all these animals down here."

The scientists had discovered an entire ecosystem!

Here were dozens of species new to science. Giant clams and mussels the size of footballs clustered near the vents. Thousands of small shrimps huddled against rocks. There were anemones, crabs, and fish. All shone brilliant white in the submersible's spotlights.

The only animals with color were colossal red-tipped tubeworms, as tall as adult humans. Bouquets of these creatures swayed in the water.

What bizarre world was this? How could so much life be flourishing in an environment so extreme to humans?

As scientists studied animal specimens from the hydrothermal vents, they made the most remarkable discovery of all. A newly discovered category of microbes, the Archaea, use energy from chemicals in some of the hot vent gases to make food. These microscopic organisms provide food for a rich, thriving ecosystem—all without the energy of sunlight.

Since 1977, scientists have explored many other vent ecosystems. Knowledge has grown along with the technology that enables people to go to previously inaccessible places. *Alvin* is still going strong, but it has been joined by a host of other submersibles. I've even helped design some of them.

Giant clam

Sunfish

THAT'S EXTREME: BIG FISH

FROM THE DEEPEST to the strangest to the most colorful, you can describe ocean life in all kinds of extreme terms. That includes biggest and gentlest. Meet some of the ocean's gentle giants.

SUNFISH

Some people call these fish "swimming heads." A sunfish looks like a large head and tail with no body in between. This circular animal is the heaviest bony fish in the world. Bony fish are the ones that you see the most—the kind with a skeleton made of bones.

So, how heavy is a sunfish? The largest one known weighed in at 5,100 pounds (2,313 kg). From fin to fin, it can grow as wide as 14 feet (4.2 m).

This fish likes to lay sideways at the water's surface like a giant saucer and bask in the sun. That's how it got its name. After soaking up some rays, it dives through the sunlit and twilight zones to feed on its favorite food—jellyfish.

Once, while in a little submarine 1,800 feet (549 m) underwater in the Florida Keys, I was surprised to see one of these strange creatures swim into view. It paused, and for a few minutes stayed nearby, apparently curious about the lights from the sub. I wondered what it must have thought about the strange creature—me—inside.

WHALE SHARK

The next time you see an 18-wheeler on the road, picture it with fins, a tail, and a sleeker shape. That gives you some idea of the size of the largest fish in the sea— the whale shark.

A whale shark, like all sharks, doesn't have bones. Instead, its skeleton is made of cartilage. That's the same tough, flexible material that forms your ears and the tip of your nose.

This gigantic fish feeds by letting water flow into its wide mouth and over its gills. The gills trap tiny plankton, which the shark swallows. It takes a lot of gulps to keep this gentle giant fed.

Whale shark

DESIGN A FISH

BY NOW YOU KNOW the ocean is full of animals of amazing shapes, sizes, and colors. Some are as cute as can be and have inspired lovable characters in animated movies. Others are some of the strangest-looking creatures imaginable—at least to humans. All of them make the ocean wondrous to explore.

Here's a fun way to further explore the ocean's diverse creatures: Design a fish! Then find out if anything like it exists.

1. Look back through this chapter at some of the ocean's inhabitants, just to get your creative juices flowing.

2. Design a make-believe fish or other sea creature. You might first want to doodle with pencil on paper to play around with different shapes. If nothing is coming to mind, look for inspiration from various animals, plants, or objects.

3. Make a model of your animal. You could make a drawing or painting, paper cutouts, or a 3D model. You might draw and color on a computer, too.

4. As you design your animal, think about where it lives, how it gets food, and what it eats. Does it have any unusual behaviors? Write down all these traits. Think about how they may affect what the animal looks like.

5. Imagine discovering this animal in the ocean. What would you call it?

6. Search through books and online with an adult's help for examples of sea creatures that resemble your designed animal in some way. Make a list of 10 animals that share at least some of your animal's traits.

QUESTIONS

- Which real animal comes closest to your make-believe animal?

- What discoveries did you make in your research? Which were the most surprising?

- Based on your fish's unique attributes, what sort of ocean environment would be best for it? How would its appearance help it survive?

FINALLY, think about this: Hundreds of species are discovered in the ocean every year. Maybe some day scientists—perhaps you—will discover one that makes you say, "Hey, I remember imagining something like that!"

Coral groupers

>>> BET YOU DIDN'T KNOW ...

That no two fish faces are alike!

Could you tell the difference between two golden retrievers? How about two tigers, two squirrels, or two eagles? Chances are, if you look carefully, you can distinguish one individual from the other. Nearly every animal has distinguishing traits that make it unique. The same is true of fish. Look at the photos of the coral groupers to the left. The groupers are orange with blue dots. But can you tell one from another? Look closely: Are patterns slightly different? Where are the dots, and how many are there? Any other differences? Every fish—like every dog, cat, bird, and human—is an individual.

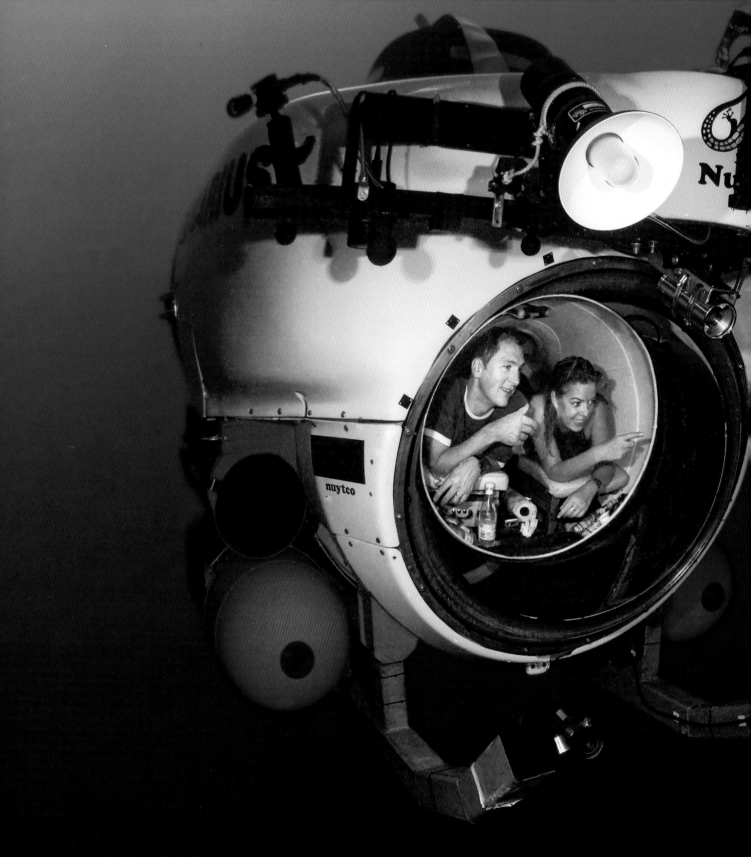

The Nuytco mini-submarine explores a coral reef off the coast of Curaçao.

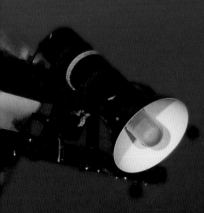

CHAPTER 3

>>> Going Deeper, Staying Longer

[AUV—Autonomous underwater vehicle;
conducts a mission without an operator

HOV—Human-occupied vehicle;
submersible that holds
one or more people

ROV—Remotely operated vehicle;
connected to a ship by cables and
controlled by an operator]

A
STROLL
ON THE
SEAFLOOR

Sylvia A. Earle in a
JIM suit off the coast
of Oahu, Hawaii

I LOOKED LIKE A
ROBOT
FROM A SCI-FI MOVIE.

I was inside a deep-sea diving suit made of metal. It was called a JIM suit, named after a diver who tested an earlier version of it in 1935.

Nearly 50 years later, the gear that encased me was made of improved materials and systems, but the idea was the same: a hard suit that could stand up to the crushing water pressure of a deep dive.

This kind of equipment had been used mostly for salvaging items from shipwrecks and making underwater repairs to offshore oil rigs. But it hadn't been part of science expeditions. Could a scientist safely use a JIM to walk on the ocean floor, make observations, collect specimens, and return to the surface? There was only one way to find out.

As I descended, the crystal blue sunlit waters faded to blue-gray and then to the darkest blue, almost black. I could barely make out the sandy bottom approaching. Then I lightly touched down at 1,250 feet (381 m). Or I should say, we touched down. The JIM suit, with me inside, was strapped to the front of a submersible containing a pilot and my friend and photographer, Al Giddings.

Usually, JIM divers are lowered and raised by a cable connected to a surface ship. But for this expedition, I hitched a ride on the outside of a submersible. When we reached bottom, the strap holding me was released, and I walked off to explore the ocean floor.

The submersible followed close behind. A slender communication line between the suit and the sub allowed us to talk to each other, but I was free to roam. As I did, I was struck by the color and variety of living things, even here in the twilight zone.

In the submersible's lights, I saw beautiful branching corals, including some known as sea fans. Different colonies were yellow, pink, orange, or black. Red crabs clung to the fans by thin legs. The scene reminded me of a beautiful flower garden.

I asked the pilot to turn off the sub's lights so that I could see all the creatures that give off their own sparkles and glows. It was like suddenly being in a galaxy of fireflies and shooting stars.

The most amazing example of bioluminescence I had ever seen occurred in a nearby field of bamboo coral. This coral grows as unbranched spirals, like giant curly whiskers or stretched-out bedsprings, each about as tall as a doorway. When I touched one with the JIM's clawed hand, something magical happened. Little rings of blue light traveled from the point of contact down to the base. If I touched near the top of the spiral, in a few seconds the light moved all the way down. I had never seen anything like it. I was spellbound.

After two and a half hours of exploring, word came from the submersible that it was time to surface. The little sub rose, pulling me up through the water by the communication line that connected us.

The expedition was a thrilling success. Not only did we show that JIM technology was a useful tool for scientists, but we also set a record. The stroll that I took on the ocean floor was the deepest that anyone has ever walked solo without a tether.

Sylvia A. Earle relaxes inside of a JIM.

Notes From the Field

MY DEEP-SEA EXPLORATION in the JIM suit took place in 1979 off the Hawaiian island of Oahu. In 2016, I revisited the site in a submersible. I was delighted to find that the corals and other life-forms were still flourishing. This time, I was able to use camera technology not yet developed in 1979. With it, we were able to capture and share beautiful images of the eerie blue light that pulses along the bamboo coral when touched.

An eXTREME Challenge

Krakatoa / Indonesia

PLANET EARTH HAS NO SHORTAGE OF EXTREME PLACES TO EXPLORE.

Fiery volcanoes, icy glaciers, dense rainforests, and towering mountains come to mind. Each presents its own set of challenges, risks, and dangers. None of these places, however, is more challenging to reach and explore than the deep ocean.

In some ways, conditions in the ocean are more difficult to overcome than those in outer space. Spacecraft don't have to withstand the bone-crushing pressures that exist in deep water. Materials in space don't have to resist corrosion from salt water. And there's certainly no need to prevent seawater from leaking into and damaging electrical systems on spacecraft.

The combination of extreme pressure, inky darkness, near-freezing temperatures, and the motions of the sea had long prevented people from exploring the ocean depths firsthand. Since early times, humans could see the stars and track the

Swiss Alps / Switzerland

An ice arch / Greenland

Te Urewera National Park / New Zealand

planets, but the depths of the sea remained unseen and unknown. That changed in the 20th century, when scientists and engineers developed the materials and other technologies needed to gain access to most of the planet—the deep sea. Now, the knowledge of how important the ocean is to everyone, everywhere, is inspiring people to look down—as well as up!

Let's take a brief journey through time to see how advances in technology opened up the ocean to exploration. Along the way, I'll show where some of my explorations fit in.

>>> BET YOU DIDN'T KNOW ...

How water pressure changes with depth!

At a depth of 33 feet (10 m), water pressure is twice what i at sea level. But you don't have to go even that deep to exp ence the change. Just swim a few feet down in a pool and can feel the pressure increase on your eardrums. Scuba c can safely go to a depth of only about 130 feet (40 m). Th the pressure is four times as great as at the surface. Dee the midnight zone, beginning at 3,250 feet (991 m), the sure would be like having an elephant stand on your thu

Modern Ocean Exploration Timeline

1837
FIRST PRACTICAL DIVING SUIT

AUGUSTUS SIEBE, a German engineer, greatly improves previous designs to develop a "heavy gear" diving suit. A copper helmet is bolted over a canvas suit and connected to the surface by an air hose. The suit is used in shallow water to salvage artifacts from shipwrecks, build tunnels, and collect sponges, pearls, and corals.

1912
TITANIC SINKS

THE WORLD'S LARGEST ocean liner of the time, the British ship *Titanic*, strikes an iceberg in the North Atlantic on its first voyage and sinks. The tragedy leads to an effort to develop a way to use sound waves to detect objects ahead of a vessel.

1830 — **1860** — **1880** — **1900** — **1920**

1868
DISCOVERY OF DEEP-SEA LIFE

CHARLES THOMSON, a Scottish naturalist, dredges part of the seafloor by lowering metal claws from the sides of two ships and scooping up sediments. In the process, he discovers life at 14,400 feet (4,389 m). At the time, most people thought life could not exist below 1,800 feet (549 m).

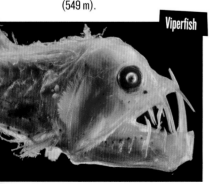

Viperfish

1872–76
FIRST MODERN OCEANOGRAPHIC EXPEDITION

RESEARCHERS ABOARD the British ship *Challenger* conduct a four-year expedition around the world. They use instruments to measure water temperature, salinity, and currents. Dredges and nets collect samples of sea life, resulting in the discovery of more than 4,000 species. By lowering a weighted line, the crew members measure ocean depths around the world. Using this method, they discover underwater mountains and other terrains.

1925
EARLY SONAR

SCIENTISTS ABOARD the German ship *Meteor* use sound waves to map the seafloor of the South Atlantic. A machine sends pulses of sound from the ship toward the seafloor. By timing how fast the sound waves bounce off the bottom of the ocean and return to the ship, scientists develop a map of the seafloor. This early form of sonar (SOund NAvigation Ranging) shows that an underwater mountain range runs through the middle of the entire Atlantic Ocean.

1934
BATHYSPHERE

AMERICAN INVENTOR Otis Barton and scientist William Beebe are lowered in a tethered spherical vessel called a bathysphere. They reach 3,028 feet (923 m) off the coast of Bermuda and discover many previously unknown creatures.

1943
SCUBA

FRENCH NAVY CAPTAIN Jacques Cousteau and engineer Émile Gagnan develop the diving gear known as scuba (self-contained underwater breathing apparatus). The gear allows divers to breathe underwater from a tank of compressed air on their back. Scuba makes it possible for almost anyone to explore coral reefs and other shallow ocean ecosystems.

1960
DEEPEST DIVE

A VESSEL CALLED a bathyscaph dives to the ocean's deepest point, a place known as Challenger Deep, in the Mariana Trench in the western Pacific. On board is Swiss engineer Jacques Piccard and Lt. Don Walsh of the U.S. Navy. It takes 4 hours 48 minutes to reach the record depth of 35,798 feet (10,911 m). The trench had been discovered during the Challenger expedition in 1875.

| 1930 | 1940 | 1950 | 1960 |

1935
ATMOSPHERIC DIVING SUIT

BRITISH DIVER JIM JARRETT tests an atmospheric diving suit designed by engineer Joseph Peress. The suit keeps the diver safe from high pressure in deep water by maintaining an internal pressure of one atmosphere—the amount of pressure experienced at sea level. Jarrett tests the suit at a depth of 404 feet (123 m).

1953
RIFT VALLEY

AMERICAN SCIENTIST Marie Tharp studies sonar profiles of the Atlantic Ocean and notices a valley running down the middle of the underwater mountain range called the Mid-Atlantic Ridge. This finding becomes evidence that the valley is where two huge sections of Earth's rocky crust, called tectonic plates, are moving apart.

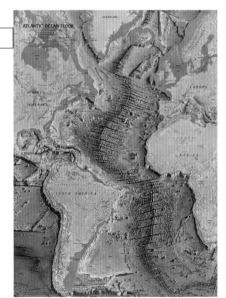

1964
SEALAB

SEALAB I, the first of three underwater habitats developed by the U.S. Navy, is lowered in place off the Bermuda coast. Throughout the 1960s, the SEALAB expeditions tested new undersea tools and diving techniques and gained knowledge about the effects on the human body of living and working on the ocean floor for long periods of time.

1977
HYDROTHERMAL VENTS

A TEAM OF GEOLOGISTS searching for hydrothermal vents near the Galápagos Islands discovers not only the vents but also robust eco-systems thriving without energy from the sun.

1968
UNDERSEA ON TV

JACQUES COUSTEAU brings the wonders of the ocean to a viewing audience in his television series *The Undersea World of Jacques Cousteau.* The series runs for eight years, following the explorations of the research ship *Calypso.*

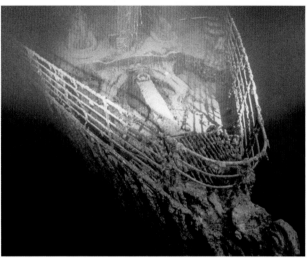

1985
TITANIC FOUND

ROBERT BALLARD leads a team of American and French scientists to locate and explore the shipwreck *Titanic* at a depth of 12,500 feet (3,810 m) on the bottom of the North Atlantic. Researchers use sonar to discover the wreck and an ROV (remotely operated vehicle) to photograph it. The following year, Ballard gets a firsthand look at the wreck in *Alvin.* Another ROV teth-ered to *Alvin* takes video of places too tight or dangerous for the sub-mersible to go.

1970   1980   1990

1970
TEKTITE II

TEN TEAMS of scientists and engineers live and work in the underwater lab Tektite II, including an all-women team that I lead. For two weeks, we explore the coral reefs and seagrass meadows in Great Lameshur Bay off the island of St. John in the U.S. Virgin Islands.

1979
SOLO DEEP-DIVE RECORD

USING THE DIVING SUIT JIM, I make several dives near Oahu, Hawaii, to explore deepwater corals. At 1,250 feet (381 m), it is the deepest solo dive in a one-atmosphere diving suit not connected to a surface platform.

1986
DEEP ROVER

FOUR OF US make record-setting solo dives to 3,281 feet (1,000 m) in the one-person submersible *Deep Rover,* a submarine that I helped develop and use to explore life in the deep sea.

1995
SATELLITE MAPPING OF SEAFLOOR

SATELLITE DATA become available for mapping of the seafloor. Satellites detect tiny bumps and dips in the ocean surface due to differences in the gravitational pull of undersea mountains, ridges, and other formations. These data are used to produce maps of the seafloor, showing that its landscape is more varied than that on the land above.

1997
AUTOSUB LAUNCHED

AUTOSUB IS THE FIRST in a series of AUVs (autonomous underwater vehicles). An AUV is a robot submarine. Its computers are programmed, telling it where to go and what to measure, without the need for a pilot or operator of any kind.

2008–09
DIGITAL SEAFLOOR MAPS

WORKING WITH National Geographic's Sustainable Seas engineers, cartographers, scientists, and many others, Google develops seafloor maps for Google Earth. The new digital maps are included in *Ocean: An Illustrated Atlas*, which I co-author with geologist Linda K. Glover.

2009
MISSION BLUE

OCEAN IN GOOGLE EARTH is launched, I win the TED Prize, and Mission Blue is formed to enlist public support for a network of "Hope Spots" in the ocean large enough to save and restore the "blue heart of the planet."

2010
CENSUS OF MARINE LIFE CONCLUDED

ABOUT 2,700 SCIENTISTS from more than 80 nations conclude a decade of research to catalog the diversity of life in the ocean. The data are stored online and made available to the public. More than 250,000 species were accounted for but more than 10 million may await discovery, not including the millions of microbial species yet to be inventoried.

2000

2010

2020

1998–2003
SUSTAINABLE SEAS

I LEAD National Geographic's Sustainable Seas Expeditions in partnership with NOAA, the Goldman Foundation, and more than 50 universities, companies, and government agencies using scuba, submersibles, ships, and ROVs to explore and document life in marine protected areas in the United States, Mexico, and Belize.

2012
SOLO DIVE TO CHALLENGER DEEP

FILM DIRECTOR and ocean explorer James Cameron reaches Challenger Deep, the deepest part of the Mariana Trench. It is the first solo dive to the bottom of this gorge on the ocean floor.

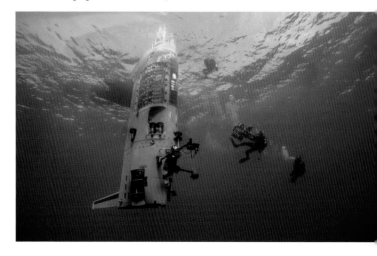

53

I LIGHTLY PRESSED THE RIGHT FOOT PEDAL WHILE ROTATING IT EVER SO SLIGHTLY.

The result was a smooth turn to the right while maintaining my depth. It was like driving a car through the ocean—a very compact car.

It was 2001 and I was piloting one of the newest submersibles in the Gulf of Mexico west of the Florida Keys. Tiny and extremely maneuverable (and fun to drive!), *Deep Worker* might be called the go-cart of subs. But this little one-person workhorse came loaded for serious research.

Standard equipment includes still and video cameras, and sonar to "see" what's ahead through murky water. A mechanical arm with a delicate touch can collect samples of live specimens.

As its name implies, *Deep Worker* was designed to go deep. On this particular dive, I was heading to 1,600 feet (488 m), well within the sub's 2,000-foot (610-m) maximum depth.

The clear acrylic dome allowed panoramic views, and I didn't want to miss a thing.

One thing I love about diving in the ocean is that I never know what I'm going to find, but I know it's going to be new and exciting.

As I slowly piloted the battery-powered sub through the sunlit zone, I noticed about a hundred reef squid, each the size of my hand, following me.

A STARLIT DRIVE IN THE DEEP

Sylvia A. Earle in *Deep Worker*

They swam in tight formation behind the sub. From outside, it must have looked like the sub was wearing a cape made of squid. When I turned, the cape turned. When I stopped, so did the cape.

The curious squid followed me into the twilight zone. Blue deepened to near black. I guided the sub to a soft landing on the seafloor. The squid were still there, but now so were many other creatures.

A crab with red eyes and long, feathery legs danced by. An animal called a giant isopod tiptoed along the muddy sand.

Reef squid / Caribbean Sea

Small lanternfish the size of my finger peered into the dome with their large eyes. The harsh lights in front of the sub hid their glittering bioluminescence. In the darkness behind me, however, I could see specks of blue-green light from tiny organs on their head, tail, and sides. The fish looked like little ships with their windows illuminated in the night.

I needed a better view of this deep-sea community. So I turned off the lights. As my eyes adjusted, the water sparkled with life. It looked like a starlit night. I had to keep reminding myself that these "stars" were not distant balls of hot gases, but living creatures only an arm's length away.

As I sat there mesmerized by the living light show, I ran my hands along the inside of the marvelous machine that brought me here. I thought about the engineers and technicians who build vehicles that make such close encounters possible.

Notes From the Field

AS I SAT IN THE DARK on the bottom of the sea, I knew that I was in a place no other human had ever been. So much of the ocean is unexplored that wherever I dive, I'm often the first person to be in that place seeing what I am seeing. Even in places that I and others have been before, there are new ways of looking, witnessing, and documenting the behavior of the animals and noting changes that occur over time.

To reach the water beneath this ice shelf, scientists melted a narrow hole and sent down an ROV.

THE ENGINEERS' WORKSHOP

Problem

How do you get a large robot packed with sensitive instruments through a hole just 30 inches (76 cm) across?

Solution

Design a robot that transforms itself!

As an explorer and scientist, I had always been interested in using new technology in my work. In college, I was one of the first researchers to use scuba equipment.

Later, I took my enthusiasm for technology to new depths. With a small group of engineers, I started a company to design and build submersibles, ROVs, and other tools to explore the deep ocean. We produced hundreds of underwater systems including the one- and two-person submersibles called *Deep Rover*.

In 1992, with my daughter, Elizabeth Taylor, I started another company, Deep Ocean Exploration and Research (DOER) Marine. This company continues to design and build underwater equipment and to solve problems related to ocean exploration.

A few years ago, scientists working in Antarctica came to DOER with a particularly challenging problem. They needed a remotely operated vehicle to explore the underside of the ice shelf that surrounds the Antarctic continent. The ice at this point is nearly 3,000 feet (914 m) thick.

Every design project has its challenges. This project had several big ones!

The only practical way to reach the ocean beneath the shelf was to melt a narrow hole through the ice

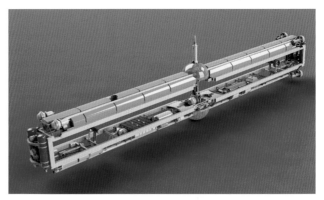

> After brainstorming ideas, engineers decided on the best way to design the SIR. They used computers to design the overall structure as well as all the parts.

> Technicians in the machine shop used computerized machines to make all the parts.

all the way to the water underneath. The ROV had to be shaped like a pencil, or a narrow tube, to fit through the hole. But once the ROV reached the water, it had to move around so that its 27 instruments could gather data.

Engineers came up with a brilliant design, inspired by toys that transform from one shape to another! Cameras, sensors, lights, thrusters, and

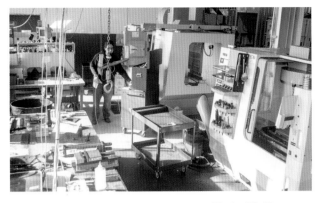

> Technicians put the parts together to assemble the SIR. If a part didn't quite fit, it had to be redesigned.

> We tested the SIR in Lake Tahoe, a deep lake along the border of California and Nevada, U.S.A. After a few final adjustments, it was ready for its missions beneath the Antarctic ice.

other instruments fold up neatly into place for the journey through the ice. Then when the vehicle reaches the water, parts fold out and the machine takes on a different shape, ready to motor through the water and gather data.

It was a simple solution—the kind of idea that engineers call elegant—but a lot went into making it work.

HERE'S HOW the Sub-Ice ROV, or SIR, transforms to do some important work beneath thick ice.

1. In the down-hole mode, the SIR is a tube 28 feet (8.5 m) long. It is narrow enough to be lowered through a hole bored in the ice.

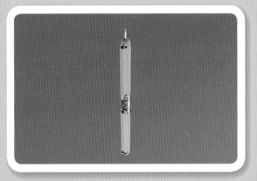

2. In the water, joints along the sides of the tube bend outward. The SIR changes shape.

3. In exploration mode, the SIR can move about and use its 27 different sensors to collect data about the water, the ice above it, and the land below it. Afterward, the ROV folds up for the trip back to the surface.

In the Works:
DEEP HOPE
& DEEP SEARCH
SUBMERSIBLES

Deep Search **will be able to travel to great depths quickly and stay submerged for many hours.**

Deep Hope **will gather data about underwater ecosystems to help scientists protect the ocean.**

DOER'S ENGINEERS
ARE DEVELOPING NEW
THREE-PERSON SUBMERSIBLES

to safely take people into the deep ocean. The subs are so simple to drive that anyone can take the controls and operate the arms, cameras, and lights, guided by a certified pilot.

Deep Hope subs can dive to 3,280 feet (1,000 m) and stay for hours on the bottom. Or they can be suspended or move mid-water with the plankton, fish, whales, and other sea creatures.

The clear acrylic materials used for the pressure hulls of small piloted subs are limited to 3,280 feet. To go to full ocean depth—36,000 feet (11,000 m)—a clear material that becomes stronger under increasing pressure is needed: glass!

Deep Search subs with glass pressure hulls are the next step in taking people to full ocean depth. Submersibles made of metal with small ports for viewing have successfully demonstrated safe transport to the greatest depths of the sea. But new technologies are inspiring new ways of thinking.

Just as airplanes and robots evolved into spacecraft in the 20th century, new systems to explore our own blue planet are quickly becoming a reality in the 21st century. What ideas do you have that can make deep ocean exploration a reality for everyone?

Adjustable lighting and multiple cameras can adapt to different situations.

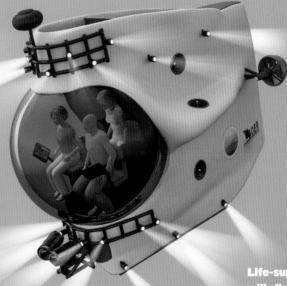

Deep Hope will have Sea Mantis manipulator arms to allow scientists to retrieve samples.

Life-support systems will allow three people to remain underwater for up to 96 hours.

Deep Search has a sleek design that will allow scientists to quickly reach the most extreme depths of the ocean and maneuver easily.

Deep Rover

Notes From the Field

DESIGNS OF HIGH-TECH VEHICLES and tools usually begin in a very low-tech way—as doodles on paper or a whiteboard. In a restaurant at breakfast one morning, I was meeting with the engineer who had designed the manipulator arms of the JIM suit. We started discussing some ideas for a one-person submersible. The engineer began sketching on a piece of paper. That sketch eventually became *Deep Rover*.

AQUARIUS UNDERWATER LABORATORY

THIS RESEARCH LAB SITS ON THE OCEAN FLOOR

66 feet (20 m) below the surface near a coral reef in the Florida Keys National Marine Sanctuary. Officially called the Aquarius Reef Base, it is one of only a few undersea research labs in the world. It serves as a base for up to six aquanauts. Most missions last about 10 days, during which marine biologists swim among the wildlife, conduct experiments, and study the health of the reef. NASA astronauts train here to simulate isolation and weightlessness in space.

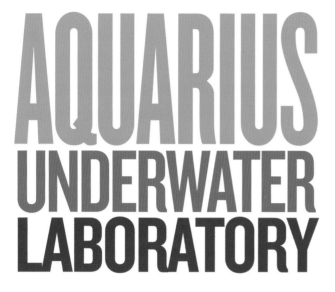

A scientist waves from inside Aquarius.

Aquanauts based in Aquarius can sample and observe marine life.

Diving down to Aquarius

NASA astronauts train at the Aquarius Reef Base.

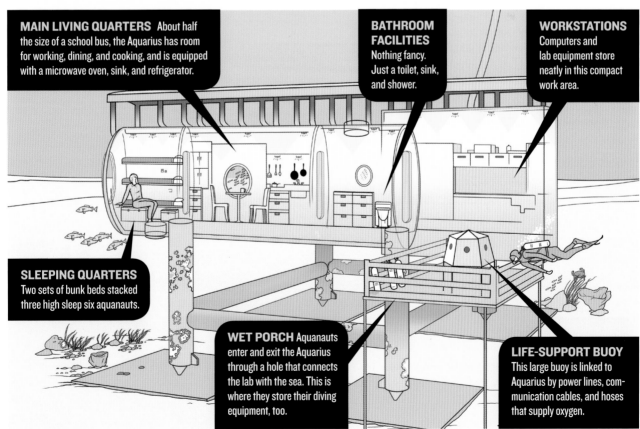

MAIN LIVING QUARTERS About half the size of a school bus, the Aquarius has room for working, dining, and cooking, and is equipped with a microwave oven, sink, and refrigerator.

BATHROOM FACILITIES Nothing fancy. Just a toilet, sink, and shower.

WORKSTATIONS Computers and lab equipment store neatly in this compact work area.

SLEEPING QUARTERS Two sets of bunk beds stacked three high sleep six aquanauts.

WET PORCH Aquanauts enter and exit the Aquarius through a hole that connects the lab with the sea. This is where they store their diving equipment, too.

LIFE-SUPPORT BUOY This large buoy is linked to Aquarius by power lines, communication cables, and hoses that supply oxygen.

James Cameron in the *DEEPSEA CHALLENGER*

ON MARCH 26, 2012, James Cameron squeezed himself inside a space little more than three feet (0.9 m) across. A short time later, he began a two-and-a-half-hour journey to the deepest point on Earth—Challenger Deep.

Though known primarily as a film director, Cameron is passionate about science and exploration. And diving to the deepest place in the ocean had been a lifelong dream. Following his dream, he led a team of engineers, scientists, and technicians that produced a submersible unlike any other.

Called *DEEPSEA CHALLENGER,* the sub was the result of years of designing, building, and testing. It was made mostly of materials that weren't even invented the first and only other time humans had reached this point—the 1960 expedition of Trieste. That vessel stayed on the bottom for only 20 minutes and had no ability to take photos or samples.

In *DEEPSEA CHALLENGER,* Cameron explored the ocean floor for three hours. He used high-definition 3D cameras to capture video of the sea life including some species never seen before. Much of the captivating footage appears in a movie that he made called *DEEPSEA CHALLENGE 3D.* It was personally a joy knowing that the sub's manipulator arm was designed by DOER— and on its wrist was a special Rolex watch that kept perfect time.

Cameron became the first person to dive alone to the deepest part of the sea. However, he says, "The quest was not driven by the need to set records, but by the same force that drives all science and exploration—curiosity."

EXPLORE THE DEEP

NOW THAT YOU'VE GOTTEN your feet wet with ocean exploration, dive deeper with these activities.

EXPERIMENT WITH WATER PRESSURE

Poke two holes in a recycled plastic bottle. One hole should be about a third of the way from the top and the other about a third of the way from the bottom. Cover the holes with masking tape, and then fill the bottle with water. Place the bottle in a sink and remove the tape. Observe the streams of water. Then answer these questions:

1. How does pressure explain the difference in the two streams of water?

2. How does this experiment show one of the challenges of exploring the deep sea?

DESIGN A SUBMERSIBLE

Submersibles come in all shapes and sizes. Some are mostly clear spheres, some are domed, and some even look like airplanes or fish. To a large degree, the design depends on the sub's criteria and constraints—what the sub needs to do and what its limitations are.

Try your hand at engineering by designing a submersible. Think about what you want the sub to do. Where do you want to explore? How deep? For how long? What kinds of instruments and equipment must it have? Do you want to be able to collect specimens and samples?

When you have decided what your sub can and cannot do, start visualizing it. Make some preliminary sketches. After you have settled on the design you want, make a final labeled drawing in color. Maybe build a 3D model of it, too. Then explain to a friend or family member how you might use your submersible to explore the ocean.

CREATE A FUTURE TIMELINE

Look back at the timeline in this chapter. Think about how ocean exploration technology has changed and how it might change further.

Then, on a sheet of paper or a computer, extend the time-line from today to a hundred years in the future. Check online with an adult's help for the latest developments in ocean exploration and imagine what events might take place in the coming years. Mark them on the timeline. Be sure to include yourself in some of the events. After all, the future is yours to explore!

Smoke rises from surface oil
being burned by cleanup crews
in the Gulf of Mexico, near
Louisiana, U.S.A.

CHAPTER 4

>>> An **Ocean** in Trouble

X

[CORAL BLEACHING—The dying of corals due to warming water and other stresses DESTRUCTIVE FISHING—Catching fish at a faster rate than they can breed, destroying habitats and catching animals unintentionally (also known as bycatch)]

In 1989, the tanker *Exxon Valdez* ran aground in Prince William Sound, in Alaska, U.S.A., spilling millions of gallons of oil into the sea.

AN OUTRAGEOUS CATASTROPHE

I WAS BOTH ANGRY AND HEARTBROKEN.

The crab that I held in my hands could barely move. It wasn't old. It wasn't diseased. It was smothered in black, tarry oil.

So were hundreds of thousands of other animals. Seabirds that had unknowingly landed on oily waters couldn't free their wings of the thick, sticky substance. The more they tried, the more they became blanketed with the stuff. Many suffocated and died, their lifeless bodies washed up on the rocky beaches.

A similar fate struck fish such as salmon and herring, as well as otters, seals, even mighty orcas.

What had happened?

A few minutes after midnight on March 24, 1989, human error had caused the oil tanker *Exxon Valdez* to plow into rocks hidden beneath the surface waters of Alaska's Prince William Sound. The collision tore open the hull, and 11 million gallons (41.6 million L) of crude oil emptied into the sea.

Equipment to begin containing and cleaning up the oil did not arrive until 24 hours after the accident. By then, the oil had already spread for miles. It crept onto the shores of the mainland and nearby islands. It coated rocks and soaked deep into sand and soil. Pushed by currents, tides, and storms, the oil eventually covered 1,300 miles (2,092 km) of coastline and a patch of ocean a little bigger than the size of Lake Erie.

Images of oil-soaked wildlife, dead or dying, hit the news. The public was outraged. So was I.

I was one of the scientists who traveled to the site to assess the damage. I was horrified by what I saw. But I was struck even more by what I didn't see, even though I knew it existed.

Out in the ocean, countless tiny planktonic organisms had been killed. With the loss of so many living things, I felt an incredible sadness. But I knew the situation was even worse. These organisms provide

ABOVE: An otter rescued from the *Exxon Valdez* spill recuperates at the Valdez Sea Otter Rescue Center.

BELOW RIGHT: Rescue workers clean a loon soaked in oil from the *Exxon Valdez* disaster.

food that suddenly was no longer available to animals that depend on it. If a small fish, snail, or other animal did eat an oily bit of algae, the oil poisoned its body. The poison collected in larger animals that ate the smaller ones, and on and on up the food chain.

That's the thing about an environmental disaster. It affects entire ecosystems in ways that aren't always noticeable.

In the weeks and months that followed, rescue workers cleaned off hundreds of birds, otters, and seals, and nursed them back to health. Cleanup crews hosed off rocks. They used floating booms to corral the oil and machines to suck it up like a vacuum cleaner. They sprayed the water with a chemical that breaks up the oil and makes it sink.

These actions wiped away most of the visible signs of the oil spill but, decades later, the oil remains just a few inches below the surface in many places. Some species, like the sea otter, have begun to recover, but their social structure has been disrupted. Animal families and communities have been torn apart. For the survivors, life will never be the same.

The *Exxon Valdez* spill, and the ones that would come after it, are grim reminders that human actions affect the ocean and the lives that depend on it, including ours.

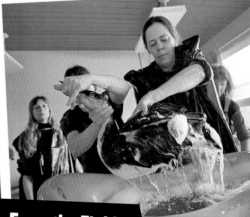

>>> BET YOU DIDN'T KNOW ...

What was done to help prevent oil spills after *Exxon Valdez*!

After the catastrophe, the U.S. Congress passed a law called the Oil Pollution Act of 1990. It clarifies who is responsible for damages from oil spills and sets procedures for cleanup. It also requires new tankers operating between U.S. ports to be double-hulled. These ships are built with two watertight hulls separated by a few feet of space. Oil is stored within the inside hull, making the oil less likely to spill out during an accident.

Notes From the Field

DURING MY SURVEY of the damage in Prince William Sound, on an island 30 miles (48 km) from the spill, I found patches of herring eggs that had washed up on shore. My colleagues and I collected eggs from various places along the beach and gave them to NOAA

OUR WORLDWIDE
GARBAGE DUMP

A loggerhead sea turtle entangled in garbage. Many of them die, but this one was found alive.

I WAS HOVERING ABOVE THE
OCEAN FLOOR

in *Deep Rover*, more than 1,000 feet (305 m) down, when a sparkle from the muddy sand caught my eye. What strange new bioluminescent creature was this? With great anticipation, I inched the sub closer ... closer ... just a little more ...

It was a soda can.

The shiny aluminum had reflected *Deep Rover*'s headlights. I was disappointed and disgusted, but I can't say I was surprised.

Over the last 40 years, I have seen trash in the sea on every single dive. Sometimes it's as small as a bottle cap or loops of lost fishing line. Sometimes it's as large as a tire or a whole car. The sad truth is, the ocean has become the world's garbage dump.

For centuries, people simply thought the ocean was so immense that they could throw anything into it without causing long-lasting harm. We were wrong. We have learned that the combined wastes from billions of people have pushed the ocean to its limits.

Millions of tons of garbage enter the ocean every year. How does it get there? Much of it is deliberately

Container ship

Crete, Greece

dumped there, but rivers also carry large amounts of trash and toxins into the sea.

Just look at a map. Follow the squiggly blue lines that represent streams and rivers and see where they lead. Most of these waters eventually make their way to the ocean. So do a lot of things that are tossed into the waterways. A burrito wrapper thrown in a creek might float from the creek to a small stream to a small river to a larger river, and end its journey in the ocean.

Some items take a more direct route. Cargo ships lose hundreds, sometimes thousands, of containers every year to storms at sea. When one washes overboard, the container and its contents add tons more trash to the ocean.

Some polluting of the ocean has been done on purpose. Until recent years, crews on trade ships, cruise ships, and military vessels were allowed to throw their garbage overboard at sea—and they did. International laws now prevent most ocean dumping.

Laws can't control the wind, though. Breezes blow paper, plastic bags, and other lightweight items from land to sea.

Any trash or garbage that ends up in the ocean is pollution. But not all pollutants are equal. Food scraps, for instance, are biodegradable. So is paper. Microorganisms break down these materials the same way they break down dead creatures in the sea. Even glass bottles, though unsightly and out of place in the sea, cause little harm to ocean life.

Plastics, on the other hand, are killers.

KILLER PLASTICS

OTHER THAN TOXIC CHEMICALS AND EXCESS CARBON DIOXIDE,

both of which are changing the chemistry of the ocean, the most abundant and dangerous pollutants are things made of plastic.

To a hungry sea turtle, a plastic bag floating in the water looks just like its favorite food—a jellyfish. The turtle chomps and swallows. But the bag just sits in the turtle's stomach, blocking the path of real food. In this way, many sea turtles starve to death.

Ocean animals mistake all sorts of plastic objects for food, with deadly consequences. Seabirds have been found with stomachs full of cigarette lighters, bottle caps, plastic foam, and toy soldiers.

Seabirds, such as albatross, even feed bits of plastic to their chicks. Little plastic spheres called nurdles are melted and shaped into plastic products, but these tiny pellets spill into the sea and look just like fish eggs. Young albatross chicks often die with their bellies full of nurdles and other plastic debris.

Plastic presents other dangers. Lost fishing nets and lines drift in the sea ... until a seal, dolphin, crab, or other animal gets tangled in the webbing. They usually can't untangle themselves or break free from the strong plastic. Many suffocate. Others starve

because they can't move well enough to catch prey. Some die from infections caused by wounds when the plastic cuts deeply into their skin.

The same tragic events happen with plastic six-pack rings. These convenient carriers for bottles or soda cans are death traps in the ocean.

Since 1989, it has been illegal to dump plastics into the ocean. But it still happens—from wind or accidents or storms washing trash from the land into the sea. Plus, most of the plastic waste that was dumped before 1989 is still there.

So what can we do about it? Laws are part of the solution. But there are a lot of ways that everyone can help, as you'll see in the next chapter.

>>> BET **YOU** DIDN'T KNOW ...

How long plastic lasts in the ocean!

It depends on the item. A thin plastic shopping bag lasts about 20 years. But scientists estimate a plastic bottle can remain intact for about 450 years! Eventually, plastic goods break down into small pieces, but they do not go away. As microplastics (pieces of plastics smaller than 5 mm), they are swallowed by small fish and other animals and continue to cause harm.

Nurdles

Hungry sea turtles often mistake plastic bags for jellyfish.

TAKING
WILDLIFE
FROM THE
SEA

THE OCEAN IS
IN TROUBLE not only from what

we put into it but also from what we take out.

People have taken fish and other wildlife from
the sea throughout history, but traditional fishing
methods have been overwhelmed by the use of new
technologies that have dramatically increased the
amount of life we are extracting from the sea.

Fleets of industrial-scale vessels are operating in
large areas of the ocean that have never before been
fished, including the waters around Antarctica, the
high seas (waters beyond national boundaries), and
deep-ocean systems everywhere.

The numbers of fish taken are staggering. The
worldwide catch is about 240 billion pounds (109
million t) per year. That's as many as 2.7 trillion
individual fish—from top predators such as tuna
and sharks to small fish further down the food chain,

such as sardines and anchovies. Like songbirds,
eagles, owls, lions, tigers, and elephants, each fish
is an individual. Like other wild animals, they are
"wildlife."

Most of this wildlife ends up on dinner plates
at restaurants or in the seafood section of grocery
stores. About a fourth of the catch is pressed for
fish oil or dried and ground up to feed chickens,
pigs, cattle, and other livestock.

The world's appetite for ocean wildlife is greater
than ever. But the ocean has only so much to give.
During the last 50 years, populations of fish such as
tuna, cod, swordfish, and halibut have decreased by
more than 90 percent. The highly prized bluefin tuna
is in worse shape. In the Pacific Ocean, its numbers
are down 97 percent! We've pushed this magnificent
creature to the brink of extinction.

Blue fin tuna are sold at a dockside market.

Usually, fishers get more than they bargain for. When a net closes on a school of sardines, for example, it also closes on sharks, dolphins, sea turtles, and other creatures that happen to be in that spot in the ocean. Millions of baited hooks on thousands of miles of fishing lines attract many creatures other than those targeted by fishers. These unintended victims are known as bycatch. It's an innocent-sounding name for a not-so-innocent practice. The loss of these animals is not counted as part of the 109 million metric tons of "catch," but they die along with those taken to market.

I remember looking on in horror as a net opened and dumped its load on the deck of a shrimp boat. Out spilled dozens of kinds of small fish, sponges, sea stars, rays, crabs, and clams. Amid the pile of sea life jumped a few startled shrimps. The crew picked them out. The rest of the creatures, some dead and many injured, were swept overboard.

Bycatch and overfishing add to the woes of our troubled ocean. Most fishing nations have laws that limit the amount of wildlife that can be taken during the year. But the laws are not always enforced.

Over the ages, many people who live along the coast and on islands have come to rely on sea creatures for food. Most of what is taken from the sea today, however, is converted to oil, fertilizer, and animal food, or provides luxury food choices for people who live far from the sea.

Why the sharp decline? It's simple: We are taking fish out of the ocean faster than they can reproduce. And we are using methods that not only take the wildlife intended but also capture and kill many times more animals, which are then thrown back into the sea, dead.

It's like taking money out of the bank without putting any in. Eventually, you run out of money. And if we continue overfishing, eventually we'll run out of fish.

That has already happened in many places for some kinds of fish, usually close to shore. When a place is "fished out," the boats move farther into the open ocean. Today, fleets can travel all around the world. They use methods that did not exist until the 1950s, when new technologies developed for military use were adapted for industrial fishing.

Fishing trawler

73

FISHING METHODS

THE FISHING INDUSTRY catches fish in many ways. Some are destructive to habitats and wildlife populations.

TRAWLING

Description: Boat pulls a large net along the seafloor.

Intended catch (sample): Halibut, sole, shrimps

Impact: Damages seafloor habitats; large amounts of catch and bycatch

DREDGING

Description: Boat drags metal mesh baskets along the seafloor.

Intended catch (sample): Clams, oysters, scallops

Impact: Damages seafloor ecosystems; large amounts of catch and bycatch

GILLNETTING

Description: Net hangs like a curtain. Openings vary in size depending on intended catch.

Intended catch (sample): Halibut, sole, shrimps

Impact: Damages seafloor habitats; large amounts of catch and bycatch

A scalloped hammerhead shark is hooked on a longline.

LONG-LINING

Description: Boat lets out a line that is many miles long. Smaller lines with baited hooks are attached to the longline. Line is retrieved after one or more days.

Intended catch (sample): Mahi-mahi, tuna, swordfish

Impact: Large amounts of catch and bycatch

>>> BET YOU DIDN'T KNOW ...

That people hunt sharks!

Sharks have an unjustified reputation for attacking people. Popular movies portray sharks as fierce, bloodthirsty creatures. But these animals are dangerous only if provoked. Humans are rarely on a shark's menu. Sharks, however, are on the menu for many people. Shark meat has grown in popularity in recent decades, and shark fin soup, once a rare delicacy in China, has become common fare worldwide.

In a practice called finning, fishers catch sharks and cut off their fins. And what happens to the shark? It is dumped back into the ocean. Unable to swim, it sinks to the seafloor where other fish feast on it. This mighty predator becomes helpless prey.

Many countries have banned finning, but millions of sharks are still taken every year to satisfy the recently created luxury markets for meat and soup.

Who's Who / Tuna

ENCOUNTERING A TUNA UNDERWATER is a thrilling experience. All the dozen or so tuna species are sleek, streamlined, and fast-swimming.

Bluefin tuna are thought to be the fastest fish in the sea, reaching speeds of 46.5 miles an hour (75 km/h). They migrate long distances, some even crossing the Atlantic. They can weigh more than half a ton and live at least 50 years, although most are now being caught before they reach their full size or potential life span. Engineers are studying the highly efficient swimming motions of bluefins to see if they can be adapted for designs for propelling ships and submarines.

GHOST
REEF

Bleached coral / West Papua, Indonesia

I KNEW THE REEF WOULD BE DIFFERENT, BUT I NEVER EXPECTED THIS!

I was scuba diving near the site of the Tektite undersea laboratory, where I had spent two glorious weeks in 1970 living underwater, exploring the reef. Now, years later, the laboratory had been removed. And that wasn't the only thing missing.

Where were the staghorn and elkhorn corals? Where were the fish? The lobsters, reef crabs, and small shrimps?

In 1970, the reef was a healthy ecosystem, supporting a vibrant community of sponges, corals, fish, crustaceans, sea turtles, and much, much more. Now, it looked like a deserted city.

The parrotfish, butterflyfish, and schools of grazing surgeonfish were missing.

Gone also were the groupers, snappers, and rays that are part of a healthy reef system. No eels peeked out from between corals to see if a meal was wandering by—because there were no meals and therefore no eels.

The nearby island of St. John was protected as a park, but fishing continued in the adjacent reefs and seagrass meadows as it has throughout most of the Caribbean Sea. Without fish, lobsters, conchs, and crabs, coral reef systems are not complete and become vulnerable to changes in temperature and other disturbances.

The reefs need the fish; the fish need the reefs. Take either away and the other suffers.

NATURE'S SIGNAL

WHEN CORALS TURN WHITE, it's a sure signal something is wrong. It means the corals' environment is being stressed in some way. The stress might come from a decrease in salinity. It might come from a surge of sediment that clouds the water for weeks or months at a time. But usually the stress comes from warming seas.

An increase in water temperature triggers the corals to release the algae that live inside them. Through photosynthesis, the algae produce food the corals need to live. So without the algae, the corals lose their source of energy as well as their color. This condition is called coral bleaching. Within a few weeks, the corals turn white and begin to die. Worldwide, half of the shallow coral reef systems that existed 50 years ago have died from loss of reef fish and other residents, and from warming ocean temperatures.

THE OCEAN IS GETTING HOTTER.

Since 1900, the average sea surface temperature has increased by about .13°F (.07°C) each decade. That doesn't sound like much, does it? But it's enough of a change to have drastic effects around the world.

Corals notice the difference. The increasing warmth is enough to kill these animals through coral bleaching or by making them more susceptible to diseases.

Most ocean species can live and thrive only within a narrow range of temperatures. If the environment gets too warm, fish and other wildlife often migrate to cooler waters. For example, over the last couple decades, black sea bass have moved from their traditional home off the shores of North Carolina, U.S.A., and up the coast to the Gulf of Maine.

They're not the only ones. Hundreds of other species are all heading to cooler northern waters. The incoming residents interrupt the balance of their new home by competing with the native sea life for food and other resources.

So, what is causing the ocean to get warmer in the first place? You may already know part of the answer: large-scale burning of wood, gas, coal, and oil. Another part of the answer is the loss of natural carbon-capturing systems on the land (like forests) and in the sea.

WARMING OCEAN

Pollution pumps carbon dioxide into the air, raising global temperatures.

Carbon dioxide and other gases in the air trap enough of the sun's heat to make life on Earth possible. But we add more of these gases when we burn fossil fuels, like coal, gas, and oil. More carbon dioxide gas in the atmosphere traps more heat. Since 1880, the machines we use to power our world have released enough carbon dioxide to raise the average global temperature about 2°F (1.1°C). The ocean absorbs a lot of that extra heat.

The ocean also absorbs a lot of the extra carbon dioxide, the same gas that gives a soda drink its fizz. In the water, this gas changes into carbonic acid. With large amounts of excess carbon dioxide dissolving in the ocean every year, the ocean is becoming more acidic.

This change in the ocean's chemistry spells trouble for all kinds of sea life. The higher acidity eats away at the limestone skeletons of coral reefs as well as the protective shells of snails, clams, and other shellfish. In addition, the acidic waters hold less calcium carbonate—the material that shellfish and coral polyps use to build their shells and casings.

Changing temperature and chemistry also affect phytoplankton that, like trees, naturally capture carbon dioxide and release oxygen into the atmosphere. Phytoplankton have declined significantly since the 1950s, while catches of ocean wildlife have sharply increased, disrupting critical nutrient cycles.

Researchers are only beginning to unravel the many ways in which the ocean responds to a warming planet. One thing is clear, however: Every cause has an effect. And each of those effects is the cause of something else. The examples you've seen in this chapter show that the cause and effect of people's actions can lead to a parade of problems. But people's actions can also lead to solutions.

Who's Who / Sea Butterfly

THESE RELATIVES of sea snails look like butterflies as they flap two winglike structures to propel themselves through the water. Their delicate shells are usually smooth. But in the increasingly acidic waters around Antarctica, their shells are pitted and worn.

Gear & Gadgets

HOW DO SCIENTISTS MEASURE the temperature of the ocean? One way is by using a system called Argo. This system includes thousands of instruments that float in the ocean and measure temperature as well as salinity and pressure. Argo floats can be programmed to descend as deep as 1.2 miles (2 km) and take measurements at various depths. The floats drift with the currents and can be submerged for up to 10 days. At the end of this time, the floats rise to the surface and transmit their data to a satellite, which beams the data to computers on land.

ONE DAY, a team of researchers was sailing across the Pacific Ocean. They noticed something orange bobbing in the water. It was part of a laundry basket. Several minutes later, a pink dustpan drifted by. Then came some huge pieces of plastic foam followed by a knotted mess of rope and torn fishing nets.

The researchers were far out at sea, 1,000 miles (1,609 km) from any land. Was this debris from a recent shipwreck somewhere nearby, perhaps a fishing boat?

No. The debris had been in the water for years. It came from places far and wide on both land and sea. Here, in the middle of the ocean, the trash gathered and became part of the vast and growing Great Pacific Garbage Patch.

The garbage patch is a collection of marine debris, or ocean trash, that is drawn into a central area by the currents that circle the northern Pacific. How does it work? Picture a plugged sink filled with water. Sprinkle pepper on the water. Then unplug the sink. A spinning column, or vortex, forms where the water drains. The vortex pulls the flecks of pepper from the edges of the sink toward the center.

Of course, the ocean doesn't have a plug, and there's no giant vortex sucking water and objects downward, but the circular motion of the currents creates forces that pull debris toward the center.

It's quite a journey. Waves on a North American beach might drag a plastic bottle into the ocean. The bottle might wash up the next day on a nearby shore, or currents might carry it far south, then west along the Equator to Southeast Asia. From there, other currents could move it north toward Japan, then back east across the Pacific. After several years, and one or two round-trips, the plastic bottle may end up in the Great Pacific Garbage Patch.

Several garbage patches form in various places around the world, in the center of circulating currents. The patches are not huge islands of trash. Rather, most of the debris is made of tiny bits of plastic no bigger than peas. They are the result of plastic bottles, caps, bags, and foam that have broken up in the sunlight and water.

The majority of these bits lurk just beneath the surface, within arm's length. Drag a screen through the water and you're likely to pick up a few colorful plastic beads and flakes.

The size of the Great Pacific Garbage Patch is difficult to measure. Some people say it's as big as Alaska, or the entire United States. But no one knows. Two things are for sure—it's big, and a tremendous challenge to clean up.

Sylvia A. Earle points to plastic pollution.

HOW DO OIL SPILLS AFFECT SHOREBIRDS?

Workers clean oil from a pelican in **Louisiana**.

OIL SPILLS AFFECT many, many animals. Among these are shorebirds such as gulls or pelicans, which feed from the ocean's waters. Shorebird feathers naturally contain certain amounts of oils. The oils block water from soaking the bird's body, which would prevent it from flying. But when an oil spill occurs, shorebirds become covered with thick oil and can't fly because of the oil's weight. The feathers stick to their bodies, and the birds can't fluff out their feathers to keep warm. Because of this, they often die from starvation, hypothermia, or not being able to avoid predators. To help these oil-spill victims survive, volunteers wash the oil from their feathers. How? Try this activity to find out.

Workers clean oil from a guillemot in **West Hatch, Somerset, England.**

MATERIALS

- Medium or large feather (from a craft store)
- Vegetable oil
- Spoon
- Cup
- 3 bowls
- Dishwashing liquid soap
- Water
- Paper towels
- Cocoa powder (optional)

STEPS

1. Pour a few spoonfuls of vegetable oil into a cup. You might want to stir in a spoonful of cocoa powder to darken the oil. This way you can see it better and it will look more like crude oil.

2. Fill a bowl with water at room temperature. Pour the oil into the water. This represents an oil spill. The oil will float on the water.

3. Fill another bowl with room temperature water and set it aside.

4. Dip the feather into the oily water. This represents a bird landing on the oil spill.

5. Now try to clean the feather the way volunteers clean birds during a real oil spill. Squeeze some dishwashing liquid soap into the remaining bowl and fill the bowl with room temperature water. Swish the water to make suds.

6. Use your hands to try washing off the oil in the soapy water. Rinse the feather in the bowl of clean water. Repeat as necessary to get the feather clean.

QUESTIONS

- How successful were you at cleaning the feather? Do you think it is easier or harder to clean crude oil off a bird during a real oil spill?
- Cleaning birds after an oil spill washes off their natural oils as well as the oil from the spill. How do you think this affects their ability to fly and survive?

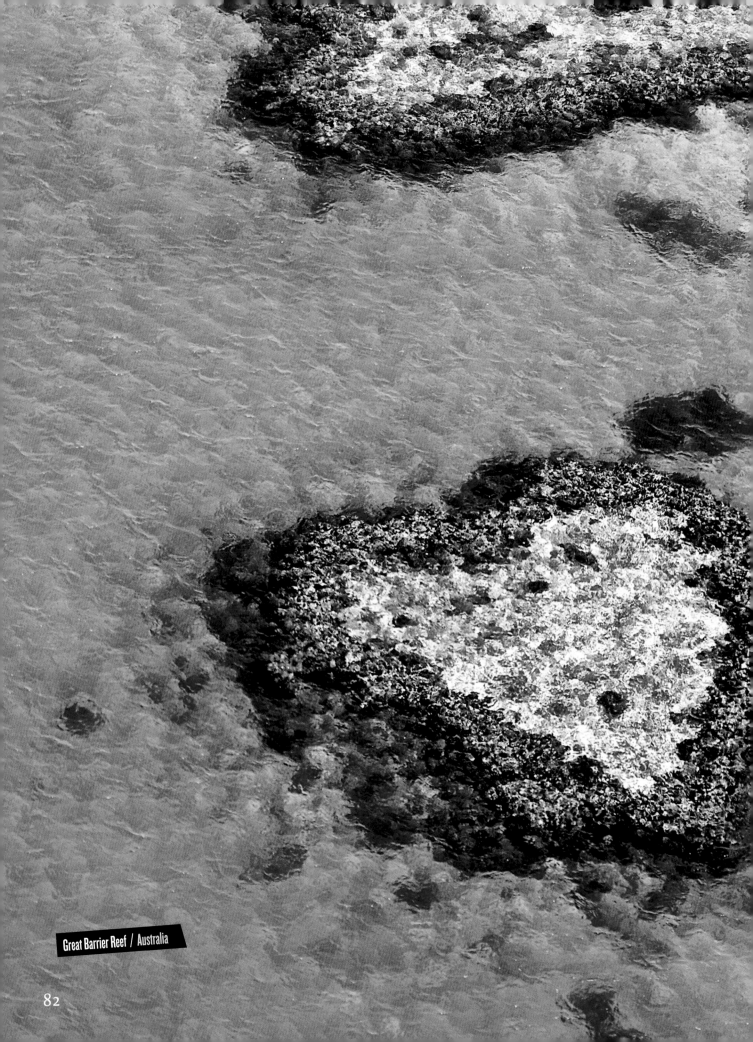

Great Barrier Reef / Australia

CHAPTER 5

>>> **How to Save an Ocean**

[HOPE SPOTS—Places in the ocean nominated for protected status because they are critical to restoring and maintaining the health of the planet SUSTAINABLE USE—Taking from natural systems without causing decline or loss of those systems and their species]

CAUGHT
GIVING BACK

I CRADLED THE SHELL IN BOTH HANDS

as I kicked downward through the crystal clear blue waters. Just ahead lay a bed of soft, green seagrass. Upon reaching it, I gently laid the shell on the grassy sand.

I waited a moment. Then out from beneath a curl in the shell slipped an eyestalk. Another peeked out next to it. The eye at the end of each stalk consisted of a black pupil ringed in yellow. The eyestalks moved back and forth, up and down. The animal had been through a stressful and bewildering experience and probably just wanted to make sure "the coast was clear." It was, now.

I swam back to the surface and climbed onto the dive boat. That's when I saw the police patrol boat heading for us. Uh-oh. This can't be good.

As the boat drew near, one of my friends began talking earnestly with two uniformed officials. They didn't appear to be in the mood for pleasant conversation.

Then I heard my friend say, "Really, officer, we were putting them in the reserve!"

By "them," she meant queen conchs. You may have seen their shells in gift shops. Their large size and glossy pink or orange interior are impressive—especially to the animals that call them home. The hard shell grows as the soft-bodied animal inside it grows, forming a spiral shape. This mollusk can live for up to 40 years, if given the chance.

But most are taken from the sea well before that. The meat has long been a traditional food for people on the islands and coasts of the Caribbean Sea and Gulf of Mexico, where the conchs live in shallow seagrass meadows and coral reefs. Tourists prize the shells as souvenirs. Pieces of the shiny, colorful interior are carved into jewelry. With such demand, conchs have been overfished, and the population has plummeted.

In efforts to save the queen conch, and the conch fishing industry, many countries in the region set aside special reserves where the conchs can be safe. Some people still take conchs even in the reserves—an illegal action called poaching.

That's what the officers thought my friends and I were doing.

A group of us were on a diving trip in the Central American country of Belize. Knowing the plight of the queen conch, we decided to start a "buy and release" program. We pooled our money and bought dozens of the animals from fishers who had recently caught them in legal waters. Then we returned them to the sea, in the reserve where they would be safe.

Who knew our good deed would almost land us in jail! Fortunately, my friend who was talking to the officers was well known in Belize for her conservation efforts. She was able to convince them that we were part of the solution, not part of the problem. We placed the rest of the conchs in the reserve.

We felt good that day. Not only because we saved a few lucky conchs, but because we saw how serious officials are about protecting them. That's cause for hope!

How the queen conch is being protected!

Efforts to protect the queen conch vary from place to place. To help give the animals a chance to recover from years of being taken in excessive numbers, it's now illegal to take queen conchs from Florida coastal waters at any time. Most other places allow some conch fishing, but with restrictions. In Belize, in addition to protected zones, conchs cannot be fished from July through September. There are limits to how many conchs can be taken in a season. Since a conch requires at least five years to mature and start to reproduce, it is easy to see how they have been so greatly depleted.

A queen conch in the Caribbean Sea

85

PROTECTING OUR LIFE-SUPPORT SYSTEM

A clownfish hides in a sea anemone.

AN ASTRONAUT FRIEND

of mine once described the space suit that he and other astronauts wear on space walks. The suit, including the backpack, is the astronauts' life-support system. It contains oxygen, water, temperature controls, and everything else needed to keep a human alive in space. During training, the astronauts learn all about this system. Then they do everything they can to take care of it. Not doing so would be foolish.

It's the same with the ocean.

The ocean is our life-support system. It provides oxygen. It drives the water cycle. It moderates temperatures around the globe. In short, the ocean keeps us alive. It's the blue heart of the planet.

So, doesn't it make sense that we learn everything we can about our life-support system? Shouldn't we do everything we can to take care of it? More and more people are answering these questions with an emphatic YES!

Recently, several thousand people met in New York City at the first ever United Nations conference devoted to the ocean. Government officials, scientists, business leaders, and concerned citizens from around the world discussed ways to improve ocean health.

Goliath Grouper

Who's Who / Goliath Grouper

THE GOLIATH GROUPER is one of the gentle giants of the sea. At eight feet (2.5 m) and 700 pounds (318 kg) when fully grown, it is an impressive fish. It's even more impressive when a group of a hundred or so goliaths gather at a reef or a shipwreck to reproduce. In a method called broadcast spawning, females release their eggs into the water as males release their sperm. The sperm fertilizes the eggs as both kinds of reproductive cells drift in the water.

In a blue world of curious creatures, goliath groupers are among the most curious. That has been part of their downfall. Divers are delighted by friendly encounters with these big fish, but curiosity also makes goliaths easy targets for spearfishers.

Notes From the Field

LAWS TO PROTECT WILDLIFE WORK, but it can be a struggle to keep them in place. Because the population of goliath groupers has increased off the Florida coast, some people want to resume fishing. That would be a big mistake. The number of groupers is still well below what it was before the species became endangered. Taking even a few can once again put them in danger of extinction.

They agreed about the need to end overfishing, reduce ocean pollution, and use the ocean in ways that are sustainable. That means using ocean resources without using them up or causing harm.

Events like the ocean conference are important because they bring people together to figure out how to solve problems. But talking must be followed by actions to bring about solutions.

Some actions include passing laws. For decades, governments have created laws to protect the ocean and its wildlife.

For instance, U.S. laws in the early 1990s banned the fishing of the goliath grouper in the Gulf of Mexico and the Caribbean Sea. This huge fish was on the brink of extinction. Now it is making a comeback. Divers come from all over the world to see and swim with these awesome creatures. The visiting divers spend money that boosts the economies of coastal towns, showing another way that fish are more valuable alive than dead.

The story of the goliath grouper shows that when it comes to solving ocean problems, humans have a partner—the ocean itself.

IMAGINE A PARK

the size of the U.S. state of Texas. Now double it! That's the size of the largest marine park in the world.

It's not the kind of park with playgrounds or hiking trails. Instead, it's a huge patch of ocean that people have agreed to safeguard as a marine protected area, or MPA. This protected area covers much of the Ross Sea off the coast of Antarctica. It's the world's largest MPA. The world's smallest is about the size of a football field. It's part of a bay used by kayakers in British Columbia, Canada.

Large or small, MPAs are intended to protect parts of the ocean from harmful human activities. The amount of protection varies. Some MPAs restrict all human entry except for scientific research. However, most MPAs allow people to use the area in ways that do not damage them, such as diving and boating. Some protected areas completely ban fishing, while others allow the managed taking of wildlife.

Governments help set up and manage MPAs. The governing body might be a country, state, province, tribe, or a seaside town. Some protected areas are a joint effort of many governments. The Ross Sea MPA is a good example. It was the result of 25 countries and the European Union (which itself has 28 member countries) working together for several years. Such cooperation is key to protecting waters far from any single nation's borders.

Around the world, various leaders have been responding to the voices of concerned citizens with a growing number of "blue parks." The small island nation of Palau has fully protected 80 percent of its ocean waters and closely manages the other 20 percent. The United Kingdom (Great Britain) has established large protected areas around some of its overseas territories in the Atlantic, Indian, and Pacific Oceans. Australia, Brazil, Canada, Chile, Colombia, Ecuador, Mexico, New Zealand, and other nations with long coastlines are taking action to safeguard

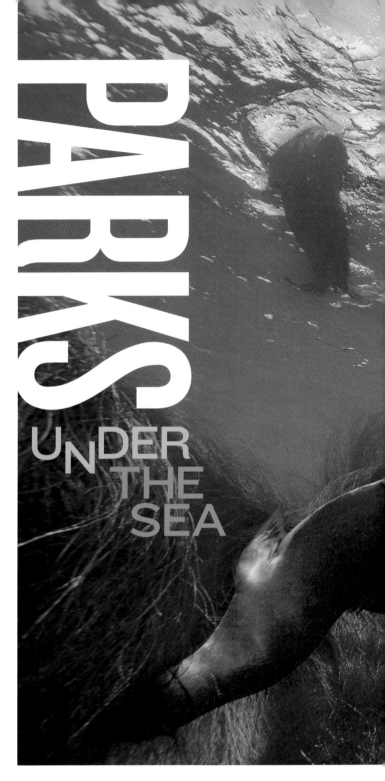

PARKS UNDER THE SEA

their living ocean treasures. Nations are increasing managed zones and places that are fully protected as "no take" or "give back" areas.

The good news about MPAs is that thousands of them are scattered across the globe. So you might think most of the ocean has effective protection. Well, that's the bad news. All of the fully protected MPAs added together in 2018 covered only about 4 percent of the vast ocean. With managed areas included,

California sea lions frolic in the underwater Channel Islands National Park, off the coast of California.

Pacific Ocean

New Marine National Monument boundary

First Marine National Monument boundary

Hawaiian Islands

Notes From the Field

LIKE MANY U.S. PRESIDENTS before him, President George W. Bush used the Antiquities Act of 1906 to designate a public park. He established what at the time was the world's largest marine protected area, the Papahanaumokuakea Marine National Monument. Ten years later, President Barack Obama quadrupled the size of that park, giving safety to ocean wildlife all the way to the edge of U.S. waters, 200 miles (322 km) offshore.

the amount is close to 8 percent. In other words, most of Earth's blue heart is not protected at all.

More needs to be done, especially for the wide, deep ocean beyond national borders. That area, known as the high seas, makes up about half of the planet. The vast open sea is owned by no single nation but is used by all. Most nations have agreed to the international Law of the Sea Treaty, which offers some general protective policies. However,

the high seas are a region of widespread "lawlessness" where piracy, large-scale destructive fishing, and other illegal activities are common.

Actions are under way to use satellites to monitor activity on the high seas. And people are working toward adopting international protective policies that would help to restore and maintain ocean health.

HOPE SPOTS

HOW CAN WE INCREASE the ocean's protected 4 percent and lower the unprotected 96 percent? One spot at a time.

I started an organization, called Mission Blue, that identifies areas of the ocean that are special in some way. I call them Hope Spots.

A Hope Spot can be special for a lot of reasons. It might have one or more of these characteristics:

- Good health ("pristine")
- A good chance of recovery
- An unusually large amount of biodiversity
- Home to rare or endangered species
- Home to species that live only in that place and nowhere else
- Historical, cultural, or spiritual importance
- Location of spectacular animal behavior, such as a migration route or spawning grounds
- Economic importance to the community

Every national park on land and every sanctuary or monument in the sea began by someone saying, "This place should be protected." That's the idea behind Hope Spots. They provide a way for even one person to get the ball rolling. Three basic steps can lead to designation as a Hope Spot.

This map shows many of the nominations for new Hope Spots across the world.

Sylvia A. Earle diving off the coast of Honduras

I-2-3 HOPE SPOTS

HERE'S HOW Hope Spots are nominated and selected.

1. NOMINATION A person or group fills out an application on the Mission Blue website explaining why a certain place should be a Hope Spot. Go to MissionBlue.org/hope-spots.

2. REVIEW A team of ocean scientists from the International Union for Conservation of Nature (IUCN) reviews the nomination to see if the place meets the criteria of a Hope Spot.

3. CELEBRATION! If the nomination is accepted, Mission Blue assists with gathering and sharing photos and other data, and spreading the word globally about the importance of the new Hope Spot. The goal is to win legal protection by gathering public support, evidence, and sound reasons for protection.

>>> BET YOU DIDN'T KNOW ...

Anyone can nominate a place to be a Hope Spot, including you!

So can a group of people, including your class or school, or clubs and other organizations. If you are passionate about protecting a certain part of the ocean, learn as much as you can about it and nominate it as a Hope Spot. Then you can share stories about your Hope Spot worldwide. With a global network of support, your Hope Spot could become the newest MPA.

So far, more than 100 Hope Spots have been approved. Some are current MPAs that need enhanced protection, but many are places that have no protection at all. You can see some of the nominated spots on the map (opposite).

WHAT WOULD BE YOUR DREAM PRESENT?

A new video game? The latest and greatest smartphone? Tickets to a concert?

For me, no present beats a trip to the bottom of the sea. And that's exactly where I celebrate my birthdays.

Once, for 11 hours, from dusk to dawn, I sat inside the one-person sub *Deep Rover* 100 feet (30.5 m) under the sea, nestled within a living coral reef. My birthday "party" was attended by the thousands of creatures that lived there.

I was in the Gulf of Mexico, just offshore from the Mexican city of Veracruz. The reef was like a city, too. But instead of buildings of glass and steel, I sat among mounds of corals and columns of sponges.

As dusk turned to twilight, the changeover of the reef residents began. Daytime creatures—wrasses, parrotfish, butterflyfish, and others—headed to their protective nooks and crannies. Out came the squirrelfish, snappers, and other carnivores of the

ON MY BIRTHDAY IN 2015, I experienced my first dive in the Arctic Ocean. As a participant in the Elysium II expedition, I joined with scientists, photographers, filmmakers, and other artists to explore and document marine life and the impacts of climate change in the far north. To stay alive in the near-freezing water, I bundled up in fuzzy underwear inside a waterproof "dry suit." The first creature I encountered was a fist-size, lavender-colored jellyfish that seemed to be made of delicate crystal, perfectly at ease, dancing next to a large chunk of floating ice. It was a reminder to me that most of life on Earth lives day and night in cold, dark water throughout their existence ... and none have to be wrapped in long fuzzy underwear!

Sylvia A. Earle snorkels in Arctic ice for the Elysium II expedition.

Coral reef / Gulf of Mexico

night. A moray eel with lacey black and white spots slid past the thick, clear dome that separated me from the water and returned repeatedly as if trying to understand who or what the strange object was that had landed in its home.

Throughout the night I watched the pageantry of life. The corals looked much like carved stone by day, but in darkness they became animated as the polyps extended their tentacles to capture plankton drifting by. The sparkles and flashes of bioluminescent creatures rivaled the glitzy lights of the port city that lit up the shoreline.

How could a reef flourish within sight of one of Mexico's most industrialized cities? The answer is simple: The reef was given a chance.

Ten years earlier, the Mexican government made the reef part of an MPA called a national marine park. Year after year, more sea life returned to this place that had been overfished. The groupers and sharks were still absent. But as the ecosystem grows healthier, they too may return. That would be the best birthday present ever.

CONNECTING WITH THE SEA

ABOUT 40 PERCENT OF THE WORLD'S POPULATION

lives within 62 miles (100 km) of the sea. Many people choose to live near the ocean, yet they sometimes go to great lengths to separate themselves from it. Walls, fences, and gates surround many waterfront developments. These structures disconnect the community from the sea.

Other people, however, are working together to connect with the sea. In the San Francisco Bay Area of the United States, for instance, a group is restoring oyster reefs.

An oyster reef is a dense collection of oysters that grow on top of one another. The reef might look like a rock formation, especially when part of it is exposed during low tide.

Oyster reefs provide plenty of benefits. They help protect shorelines from destructive waves, especially during storms. These natural "breaks" are much more effective than concrete seawalls built for the same purpose. They even clean the water by filtering out muddy sediments.

But overfishing of oysters has taken its toll. So has dredging, a method used to scoop sand and mud from

the bottom of the bay to keep it deep enough for ships. Today, only a fraction of the once expansive reefs remains.

Now, an organization called the Wild Oyster Project is doing something about it. They are partnering with local oyster farmers to rebuild the reefs. They also recruit the help of restaurants and people who eat oysters to collect and clean the shells. The shells give new oysters a hard base to latch on to. Volunteers from all walks of life become scientists when they observe and record how well young oysters are growing on the shells.

With so many people pitching in, the San Francisco Bay could become healthier for ocean wildlife—and for people, too.

Golden Gate Bridge / San Francisco, California

Oyster reef

NO COAST? NO PROBLEM!

Help organize cleanup days.

YOU DON'T HAVE TO LIVE

near the coast to be a steward of the ocean. In fact, kids are making a positive difference in our ocean's health even though they are thousands of miles from the deep blue sea.

For example, the National Oceanic and Atmospheric Administration (NOAA) has Ocean Guardian programs in which kids can get involved through their schools. Through classroom projects, students help protect the ocean, either directly or by protecting the streams and rivers that eventually flow into the ocean.

- Start school campaigns such as bike-to-school days, water-saving days, and zero waste lunch and no single-use plastic programs.
- Create school gardens using native plants.
- Organize days for cleanups of a beach, a stream, or the school grounds.
- Start a composting program to recycle the organic wastes from the school cafeteria.
- Install recycling containers around the school or community.
- Install water bottle refilling stations at school so kids can refill reusable water bottles.

Another NOAA program is Zero Waste Week. This program encourages kids and adults to "Go Green and Think Blue" by reducing waste, especially single-use plastic, such as water bottles, straws, and utensils. The program lasts only a week, but "Go Green and Think Blue" is a motto that could guide actions for a lifetime.

Young people everywhere are learning about and speaking up for the ocean. Some school groups use underwater webcams to see what's happening in real time at different places in the sea. In one project, teens used a webcam and underwater sensors to remotely monitor the conditions of the water and sea turtles in the Caribbean. The data they collected led to greater protection for these marine animals.

With adult involvement, some groups organize expeditions. They learn how to scuba dive and experience the thrill of ocean exploration firsthand. Whether helping to restore a coral reef, install webcams, or track sharks, young people get a real taste of what it's like to be a marine scientist.

Ocean clubs are popping up in schools all around the world. When I visit these groups, I'm deeply impressed by their enthusiasm, by their passion to make a difference. It's contagious!

The ocean needs champions. You can become one yourself!

Here's a small sampling of exciting projects that Ocean Guardian classrooms have put into action. Which of these might you and your classmates like to do? What other projects can you think of?

- Explore your local watershed—the land that is drained by streams and rivers in your area. Learn about the plants and animals that live along and in the waterways.
- Help restore damaged watershed habitat. For example, replace non-native plant species with native species or plant native vegetation along eroded stream banks.

WHAT YOU CAN DO

Sea lion / La Paz, Mexico

EVERYONE CAN PITCH IN TO SAVE OUR OCEAN.

It's not just up to governments and scientists. It's up to each and every one of us. It is up to me, and it is up to you.

Here are some things you can do to make a real difference in the health of our ocean and in the health of our world.

1. GET INFORMED.

You're doing that already! By reading this book, you know more about the ocean than most people do—adults as well as kids. But this book is just a start. If something in these pages has sparked your interest, learn more about it. Check out the resources section at the end of this book, or better yet, go exploring yourself!

2. GET WET!

There is no substitute for personally exploring the ocean or lakes, rivers, and streams and asking questions about the creatures that live there. Discover for yourself what is happening by looking carefully and reporting honestly what you see. This is what scientists do, and it is what you can do, too.

Reduce your carbon footprint.

3. SPREAD THE WORD.

Share what you know with family and friends. The more people know about the wonders and problems of the ocean, the more they'll care. And the more they care, the more likely they'll take action. People can't care if they don't know what the problems are.

4. DON'T LITTER, AND CUT DOWN ON PLASTIC PRODUCTS.

Whether it's a gum wrapper, a soda can, or a plastic bag, hold on to it until you can dispose of it responsibly. That will be one less piece of trash that makes its way to the ocean or any other part of the environment. Avoid plastic products—especially those that can be used only once—whenever you can. See page 102 for tips!

5. REDUCE YOUR CARBON FOOTPRINT.

Cut back on the use of fossil fuels as much as possible. Consider walking or riding a bike instead of taking a car. Turn off lights and powered equipment when not in use. Be aware of the cost to nature of your energy use. Be mindful of food choices, too, and consider the transport and other carbon costs of local versus distant sources. You can also research the carbon cost of growing plants compared to that of growing animals.

6. REMIND ADULTS TO USE LESS FERTILIZER AND AVOID USING TOXIC CHEMICALS.

A lot of toxic chemicals from homes, cities, factories, and farms wash down drains or off the land and eventually reach the ocean, where they change ocean

Volunteer with local cleanup groups.

Use less fertilizer and toxic chemicals.

chemistry. This harms life in the sea and damages Earth's basic "life-support" functions.

7. CONSUME OCEAN WILDLIFE—SEAFOOD— WITH RESPECT, AND ASK QUESTIONS.

If you choose to consume ocean wildlife, wouldn't you like to know what the fish is on your plate, where it has come from, and how old it was? There are more than 30,000 species of wild fish! What fish is in a fish taco? Or fish and chips? How old was it? You may be dining on an animal taken from the sea thousands of feet deep and thousands of miles away, one that may have been older than you, your parents, or even your grandparents!

8. VOICE YOUR OPINION.

Are you learning how to write thought pieces in school? Put that skill to use. Write letters to local leaders, manufacturers, store managers, and restaurant owners about an ocean issue. Express your ideas clearly and respectfully. Urge people to do what they can to improve ocean health. You can also take and share photographs and leave comments to internet news stories about the ocean.

9. GET INVOLVED.

Start or join a group that organizes beach or local cleanups, or one that explores or cares for wildlife. Can't find a group? Organize one with family and friends! Be sure you have permission to clean up the area. Have adult supervision and follow all safety rules.

10. LOOK IN THE MIRROR.

Everyone is different from everyone else. There is only one person who has ever been or who will ever be just like you, and that's you. What makes you special? Do you have a way with words? Are you good with numbers? Can you sing? Dance? Play music? Create art? Tell jokes? Play games? Do you have a special empathy for animals? Do you love science or engineering? Or exploring unknown places? Solving puzzles? Can you run faster than anyone else you know? What do you do well and what makes you happy? Think about those things that make you *you* and imagine how you can use your special powers to make a difference in the world—and maybe for the ocean, too.

IT'S TIME TO WAGE A BATTLE ... AGAINST PLASTIC.

As you've learned, plastic has become an enormous problem, threatening the health of the ocean, its inhabitants, and humans everywhere. It's time to make a decision: planet or plastic?

Luckily, kids like you aren't sitting back and waiting for politicians, businesspeople, or other adults to solve the problem of plastic trash in the ocean. Instead, young people are leading the way by hosting cleanups, encouraging local businesses and restaurants to cut back on plastic, and reducing their own plastic waste.

Best of all? You, too, can become a waste warrior. Take the Kids vs. Plastic Pledge at natgeokids.com/KidsVsPlastic, and find out how you can join the battle for our planet. Get started with these 10 easy tips:

1. **SAY NO TO STRAWS.** Animals can get sick after mistaking them for food. Instead, carry your own paper straw or reusable version. Try one made of bamboo, silicone, glass, or paper!

2. **FILL UP AT A FOUNTAIN.** Drink out of a reusable water bottle instead of a plastic version. That way you won't be buying one of the nearly one million plastic drink bottles sold every minute around the world.

3. **PACK A BETTER BAG.** Pack sandwiches and snacks in reusable containers or cloth sacks instead of plastic bags.

4. **SNACK ON FRUIT.** Pack an apple, banana, or orange instead of snack packs. Fruit fills you up in a healthy way, plus there's no extra packaging. (Save the core, peels, and rinds for your compost bin.)

5. **BUILD A GOOD GOODIE BAG.** Don't fill your birthday goodie bags with plastic yo-yos and other trinkets for your friends. Instead, give them home-made treats or coupons to a local bakery.

6. **GO FOR THE CONE.** No matter your favorite ice-cream flavor, always choose to have it in a cone. Who needs plastic spoons and cups when you can eat the bowl?

7. **BUY IN BULK.** Encourage your family to shop for snacks, cereal, and pasta in the bulk section of your grocery store or natural food shop to avoid waste from plastic packaging. Then store it all in reusable glass jars.

8. **DITCH MICROBEADS.** Don't use face wash or toothpaste with microbeads. (If the ingredients label lists polyethylene or polypropylene, the item likely contains microbeads.) These tiny plastic beads go down the drain, eventually flowing to rivers, lakes, and the ocean. There they can be mistaken for food by fish and sea turtles—a dish that could be deadly.

9. **NEVER LITTER.** Hey, sometimes you have to use plastic, and that's OK! But always recycle the plastic that you can, and never leave it in the environment. Trash left on the ground often blows into creeks and rivers, eventually making its way to the ocean.

10. **PICK UP WHAT YOU CAN.** Grab a parent and pick up the trash that you find in your local creek or river. But be careful: Never grab anything that looks sharp or dangerous.

Take it further by finding out how to make your own paper straws, a reusable lunch bag, and even how to organize and conduct a neighborhood cleanup. Remember: You can make a real difference. Now that's extreme!

Part of the PLANET **OR** PLASTIC? initiative

Grab a parent and help clean up your beaches.

WATER BOTTLE FILL STATION

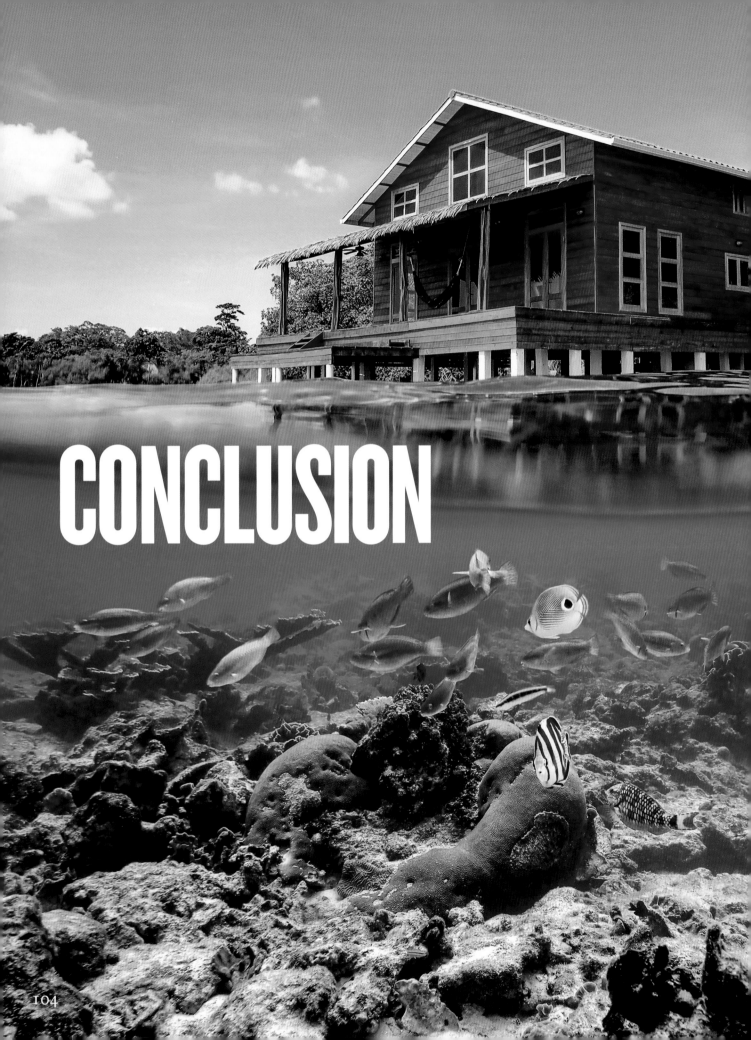

CONCLUSION

A stilt house / Caribbean

Sun star / Bird Island, Falkland Islands

I HOPE YOU HAVE ENJOYED our explorations into the blue wilderness. This book has given you a glimpse (but only a glimpse) of the marvels of the sea.

Think back. If you could have come along on any of the expeditions in this book, which would it have been? What made that expedition special to you? More important, how have your ideas of the ocean changed?

You now know that a rich array of life exists beneath the waves, a biodiversity greater than that of any ecosystem on land. You also know that the ocean floor is more varied and extreme than any landscape on shore—from the deepest, darkest canyons to mountain ranges that wind their way around the globe.

Like many people, you may have once thought the ocean was too big to harm. We now know that's not true. People's actions have damaged our planet's blue heart despite its immense size. But just as a healthy ocean is not too big to get sick, a sick ocean is not too big to get healthy. We know how to fix the problems, but we have to act now. This is the "sweet spot in time"; the decisions we make in the next few years will affect life on Earth for generations to come.

This book is filled with the thrills of exploration, but the most exhilarating thrills await you beyond these pages—in the great outdoors. As much as possible, head outside and explore our natural world. As I've suggested earlier, get wet! But even if you can't explore the ocean, a lake, or a stream, take the time to observe a bird, a frog, a butterfly, a flower. That's what I did as a kid on our farm in New Jersey, before moving to the Gulf Coast. I could spend hours watching the animals by a pond or in our backyard. I'd make intricate drawings of them. My mom used to call these times my "investigations." I just called them fun. I didn't realize it then, but I was being a scientist. You can be one, too.

So, let's get out and explore. That's what I'm going to continue to do! As you read this, I might be taking a new submersible on a test run, scuba diving to check the health of some of my favorite reefs, or exploring one of the newest Hope Spots.

Adventures await all of us. Let's share them.

GLOSSARY

Abyssal zone The fourth layer of the ocean, which includes the ocean's average depth of 13,780 feet (4,200 m)

Adaptation A characteristic that helps an organism survive in its environment

AUV (autonomous underwater vehicle) A vehicle that conducts a mission without an operator

Biodiversity The variety of living things in an ecosystem

Bioluminescence The production of light by a living organism

Coral bleaching The dying of corals due to warming water and other stresses

Coral reef An ecosystem growing on the seafloor and made up of living corals and their skeletons and many other kinds of organisms

Current A large stream of water moving through the ocean

Destructive fishing Catching fish at a faster rate than the fish can breed, destroying habitats and catching animals unintentionally (also known as bycatch)

Ecosystem The living and non-living things in an area and their interactions

Hadal zone The deepest layer of the ocean, which includes its deepest trenches

High tide The point at which the water along the shore is at its highest

Hope Spots Places in the ocean nominated for care that, if protected, will help restore and protect the health of the planet

HOV (human-occupied vehicle) A submersible that holds one or more people

Hydrothermal vent An opening in the seafloor from which heated mineral-rich water flows

Intertidal zone The area of a coastline between low tide and high tide

Low tide The point at which the water along the shore is at its lowest

Marine protected area (MPA) An area of the ocean in which human activity that is harmful to wildlife is restricted or prohibited

Midnight zone The third layer of the ocean, which is dark and cold, and in which most creatures have some form of bioluminescence

Ocean Immense body of salt water that covers nearly three-fourths of Earth's surface

Overfishing The taking of fish at a faster rate than they can reproduce, resulting in lower fish population

Photosynthesis A process by which certain organisms use sunlight to make food from carbon dioxide and water.

Phytoplankton Tiny organisms in water that use sunlight to make food

Predator An animal that hunts and feeds on other animals

Prey An animal that is hunted and killed by another animal for food

Rip current A strong narrow stream of water moving outward from a beach

Rogue wave A large wave that forms unexpectedly

ROV (remotely operated vehicle) A vehicle connected to a ship by cables and controlled by an operator

Salinity The amount of salts dissolved in water

Species A group of organisms that are similar and can mate and produce offspring which can also mate and produce offspring

Submersible An underwater craft designed for research and exploration

Sunlit zone The top layer of the ocean, where enough sunlight reaches to provide the energy for photosynthesis

Sustainable use Taking from natural systems without causing decline or loss of those systems and their species

Tide The daily rise and fall of ocean water along the shore

Tide pool A small rocky enclosure along the coast that traps water and sea life during low tide

Trench A long, narrow canyon on the ocean floor

Tsunami A large wave or series of waves caused by an earthquake on the seafloor or some other major disturbance

Twilight zone The second layer of the ocean, where little sunlight reaches and in which great migrations take place nightly as animals from greater depths swim upward to feed

Water cycle The continuous movement of water through the environment as a gas, liquid, and solid

Watershed The land that is drained by streams and rivers in an area

Wave The movement of energy through water

Humpback whale

A diver with a hybrid remotely operated vehicle (HROV) off the coast of southern France

RESOURCES
& FURTHER READING

HERE ARE MORE WAYS TO EXPLORE THE OCEAN:

- Read more about the ocean's incredible array of life in these books by Sylvia A. Earle: *Sea Critters; Coral Reefs;* and *Hello, Fish! Visiting the Coral Reef.* And if you'd like to learn more about Sylvia's explorations, you'll enjoy the book *Dive! My Adventures in the Deep Frontier.* You'll feel like you are diving with Sylvia as she tracks whales, lives in an underwater lab, and more. Also be sure to check out *Sea Change, The World Is Blue, Wild Ocean, Illustrated Atlas of the Ocean,* and *Blue Hope.* You'll find more information on the ocean and gorgeous, inspiring photographs.

- The internet is your doorway to all sorts of information, games, activities, and videos about the ocean and its wildlife. Grab a grown-up to start your explorations at oceanservice.noaa.gov/kids.

- Do you want to keep up with some of the latest technology for exploring the ocean? With an adult, check out what's new at the engineering company Sylvia started—Deep Ocean Exploration and Research, or DOER: doermarine.com/.

- Do you remember reading about Sylvia's memorable stroll on the ocean floor in the JIM suit? She witnessed how rings of blue light travel along the spirals of bamboo coral when the coral is touched. Grab a parent to witness this mesmerizing event here: petapixel.com/2016/09/13/first-ever-hd-video-bioluminescent-coral-shot-4m-iso-canon-camera/.

- Learn how kids are working together in school to help save the ocean. With an adult's permission, learn about existing projects and get ideas for projects you can do in your own school at this site: sanctuaries.noaa.gov/education/ocean_guardian.

- Of course, National Geographic has tons of fun and interesting videos, photos, magazines, and even more books on the ocean here: natgeokids.com.

INDEX

Harbor seal in kelp forest / Cortes Bank, California

A NASA astronaut trains with *Deep Worker* off the coast of Florida.

PHOTO CREDITS

Dolphins

Emperor penguins

There's more to SEE in the SEA!

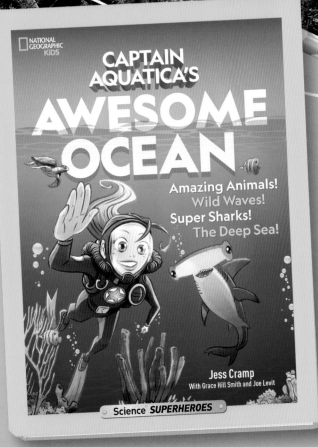

Take a deep dive into all the realms of the ocean with shark researcher and marine conservationist Jess Cramp. This fun, fascinating, and fact-filled book combines real science with comic book flair.

IF YOU LIKE GOING TO EXTREMES, CHECK OUT MORE BOOKS IN THIS EXCITING SERIES!